TAKING CONTROL
OF YOUR CAREER

A Handbook for Health Professionals

GAIL J. DONNER | MARY M. WHEELER

TAKING CONTROL OF YOUR CAREER

A Handbook for Health Professionals

GAIL J. DONNER, RN, PhD
MARY M. WHEELER, RN, MEd, PCC

MOSBY

ELSEVIER

Library and Archives Canada Cataloguing in Publication
Donner, Gail J. (Gail Judith), 1942–
   Taking control of your career: a handbook for health professionals / Gail J. Donner, Mary M. Wheeler.
Includes index.
ISBN 978-1-897422-16-8
   1. Medicine—Vocational guidance.   2. Medical personnel.
3. Career development.   I. Wheeler, Mary M.   II. Title.
R690.D65 2008   610.69   C2008-904319-7

Vice President, Publishing: Ann Millar
Managing Developmental Editor: Martina van de Velde
Managing Production Editor: Roberta A. Spinosa-Millman
Copy Editor: Liisa Kelly
Cover Design: Brett J. Miller
Interior Design: Monica Kompter
Typesetting and Assembly: Jansom
Printing and Binding: Transcontinental

Elsevier Canada
905 King Street West, 4th Floor
Toronto, ON, Canada M6K 3G9
Phone: 1-866-896-3331
Fax: 1-866-359-9534

Printed in Canada
1 2 3 4 5   13 12 11 10 09

Working together to grow
libraries in developing countries
www.elsevier.com | www.bookaid.org | www.sabre.org

ELSEVIER   BOOK AID International   Sabre Foundation

About the Authors

Betty Milne

Gail J. Donner, RN, PhD and *Mary M. Wheeler,* RN, MEd, PCC are partners in **donnerwheeler**, a consulting firm specializing in individual and organizational career planning and development programs and services, with clients in Canada, the United States, Europe, and South Africa. Although Gail and Mary began their work with nurses, over the past 10 years their clients have grown to include a broad range of health professionals. This handbook is the result of conversations and feedback from those health professionals who repeatedly asked for a resource to help them with their careers.

Gail is Professor and Dean Emeritus of the Lawrence S. Bloomberg Faculty of Nursing at the University of Toronto. Her research and consulting interests include career development, health policy, and nursing administration. In addition to presenting papers, seminars, and workshops on a variety of health care topics, Gail has been active on a number of boards and committees. She is currently a member of the Board of Trustees of the Hospital for Sick Children and Chair of the Board of The Change Foundation, both in Toronto, Canada. Gail is also a member of the Board of HealthyKids International and book editor of the *Canadian Journal of Nursing Leadership*. For her contributions to nursing and the community, Gail has received the Order of Ontario, an honourary Doctor of Science from Ryerson University, the Registered Nurses' Association of Ontario Award of Merit, the YWCA Woman of Distinction Award, and the Ontario Medical Association Centennial Award.

v

Mary is a certified coach with over 15 years of consulting experience in career, organization, and human resource development, and has published extensively in the areas of career development, coaching, and mentoring. In addition to her work with **donnerwheeler**, Mary has co-led CareerCycles Getaways for the Ontario Medical Association Physician Health Program and acts as an executive coach in her role as an associate of Development by Design. Mary is an active member of the International Coach Federation, the Association of Career Professionals International, and the Career Planning & Adult Development Network, for which she has been a book reviewer. Mary also reviews book proposals for Sigma Theta Tau International. Mary is currently a member of the Nursing Advisory Committee of Ryerson University, and also a member of the International Council of Nurses Bank of Nurse Experts in the field of Human Resources Planning & Development and Nursing Remuneration–Working Conditions.

Reviewers

Carol Cameron, RM, MA

Head Midwife, Division of Midwifery
Department of Obstetrics and Gynecology
Markham Stouffville Hospital
Markham, Ontario

Peter Coughlin, MSW, RSW

Instructor, Department of Family Medicine
Queen's University
Instructor, Social Service Worker Diploma Program
St. Lawrence College
Kingston, Ontario

Michael McGillion, RN, PhD

Assistant Professor
Lawrence S. Bloomberg Faculty of Nursing
University of Toronto
Toronto, Ontario

Melanie Morris, MEd, RD

Professional and Education Leader, Clinical Nutrition
Sunnybrook Health Sciences Centre
Toronto, Ontario

Diem Tran, BScPT, MSc (Cand.)

Lecturer, Graduate Department of Rehabilitation Sciences
University of Toronto
Toronto, Ontario

Acknowledgements

Working with others has added immensely to the strength of this book, and to our joy in writing it. We want to thank Ann Millar, Vice President of Publishing at Elsevier, for her confidence in us, and for her willingness—once again—to take a chance on something that began as an idea; her support from inception to production has been invaluable. This book has developed from the great success of *Taking Control of Your Nursing Career*, published by Elsevier in 2004. *Taking Control of Your Nursing Career* was a group effort by a number of colleagues, and we want to thank Sue Bookey-Bassett, Michelle Cooper, Claire Mallette, Linda McGillis Hall, Janice Waddell, and Margot Young; their work helped form the foundation for this current book, and we remain forever grateful for their insights, knowledge, and contributions.

Because we wanted this book to be relevant and useful to our colleagues in the health professions, we asked a wide group of professionals to act as our "reality check," to read the outlines and various drafts, and to offer their guidance. We want to thank Karin Carmichael, Raquel Figueroa, Sandra Grgas, Lori Issenman, Catherine Nicol, Christiaan Stevens, and Anne Symes for their generosity, for the time they took in helping us, and for their enthusiasm for this project. As well, thanks to Merle Ballaigues for her assistance in reviewing the self-assessment tools. We also appreciate the reviewers, who provided candid, thoughtful, and comprehensive feedback, and who helped immeasurably in creating a work of which we can be proud.

Thanks to Martina van de Velde for her excellent work as our Developmental Editor, to Liisa Kelly for her superb editing, to Roberta A. Spinosa-Millman, Managing Production Editor, for her help, and to Angela Smith for her marketing expertise and advice. Early in this work, Barbara Bauer, who has worked with us on many, many projects, provided excellent editorial advice; as always, we appreciate her skill, her expertise, and her commitment to our work.

Our families are wonderful! They have stood behind every idea we have had, and every project we have undertaken. Gail wants to thank Arthur for his patience and love, to thank Elizabeth, Derek, and Simon for their enthusiasm, and to thank Theo and Ben for keeping her grounded. Mary extends her heartfelt thanks to her family and friends who encircle her with love, support, and encouragement. And finally, we could not have done this without each other.

CONTENTS

Part 1   Taking Control of Your Career:
An Introduction   1

    How to Use This Handbook   4

Part 2   Key Issues in the Current Health Care
Environment   7

    Health Human Resources   8

    Technological Advances   9

    Chronic Illness and Health Care in
the Community   10

    Focus on Safety   11

    Multi-Generational Diversity   11

    Interprofessional Education and Practice   12

    Professional Responsibility   13

    References   13

Part 3   Planning Throughout the Major Stages
of Your Career   15

    The Career Continuum   15

    Recognizing Opportunities and Challenges
During Major Periods of a Health Career   17

    The Early-Career Professional   17

    The Mid-Career Professional   19

    The Late-Career Professional   21

    Where Do I Go From Here?   23

    References   24

Part 4   Using the Donner–Wheeler Model to Plan Your Career   25

PHASE ONE Scanning Your Environment   31
What Is Scanning?   31
Why Is Scanning Important?   31
How to Do a Scan   32
Activity 1: Scanning Your Environment   33
What Have You Accomplished?   35
What Is Your Next Step?   36

PHASE TWO Completing Your Self-Assessment   37
What Is Assessing?   37
Why Is Assessing Important?   38
How to Do a Self-Assessment   39
   Assessing Your Values   40
   Assessing Your Knowledge and Skills   41
   Assessing Your Interests   42
   *Recognizing and Acknowledging Your
      Accomplishments*   43
Activity 2: Completing Your Self-Assessment   44
Asking for Feedback: Doing a Reality Check   52
How to Complete Your Reality Check   52
Activity 3: Completing Your Reality Check   53
What Have You Accomplished?   55
What Is Your Next Step?   57

PHASE THREE Creating Your Career Vision   59
What Is Visioning?   59
Why Is Visioning Important?   60
How to Create Your Career Vision   61

Activity 4: Creating Your Career Vision   62

Self-Limiting Beliefs   66

Activity 5: Self-Limiting Beliefs   67

What Have You Accomplished?   68

What Is Your Next Step?   70

PHASE FOUR Developing Your Strategic
Career Plan   71

What Is a Strategic Career Plan?   71

Why Is Planning Important?   72

How to Develop a Strategic Career Plan   73

    Setting Your Career Goals   73

    Formulating Your Action Steps   75

    Identifying Your Resources   75

    Establishing Your Timelines   76

    Identifying Your Indicators of Success   76

Activity 6: Developing Your Strategic Career Plan   77

What Have You Accomplished?   78

What Is Your Next Step?   80

PHASE FIVE Marketing Yourself   81

What Is Marketing?   81

Why Is Marketing Important?   82

The Product Is You!   82

Networking   83

Finding a Mentor   84

Marketing Yourself in Writing   85

    Résumés   85

    The Cover Letter   86

    What Is the Difference Between a Résumé
      and a Curriculum Vitae?   86

    Business Cards   87

    Web Sites, Blogs, and Writing for Publication   87

Marketing Yourself in Person   88
   The Interview   88
   Making Presentations   89
   Acting as a Mentor   90
Activity 7: Marketing Yourself   91
What Have You Accomplished?   92
What Is Your Next Step?   93

Part 5   Sustaining Your Career Plan   97

Appendix A: Assessment Tools   101

Appendix B: Résumé Tips   105

Appendix C: Outline for a Curriculum Vitae (CV)   109

Appendix D: Interview Tips   113

Appendix E: Coaching and Mentoring—Key Elements   117

Appendix F: Selected Further Reading   119

Index   123

Part One

Taking Control of Your Career: An Introduction

> *Today, a career is a life expression of how a person wants to be-in-the-world.* Frederic Hudson

Being a health professional in Canada, and indeed anywhere in the world, is challenging from many perspectives. Changes in education, professional practice, legislation and regulation, and systems and structures are no longer unusual, and volatility seems to be a permanent fixture. The past several years have been marked by incredible technological change, an increased demand for a diverse range of services, looming shortages of health professionals, and increasing fiscal challenges. At the same time, we have created new roles, new work settings, and a new focus on interdisciplinary teams and collaborative work. Although challenges remain, the ways that the health care world has changed have created opportunities for a diverse range of people who seek careers in health care.

Careers, whether in health care or any other profession, move along a continuum that begins when we first decide to enter an educational program that will prepare us for the world of work. From here, following a period in the first years of employment where we aim to determine that we are in the right place and doing the right thing, we pass through a number of years where we grow and develop, making our most significant contributions to a profession. The cycle ends when we finally withdraw and begin to consider opening a new chapter in our lives, perhaps in a new line of work, a variation of our previous career, or retirement. Whether you are beginning your career in health care, moving into your prime, or contemplating retirement, the paths to success and satisfaction are varied and often complex. Now, the work environment provides a number of options that increase exponentially as you gain experience and expertise. It is now very likely that you will not finish your career in the same place and with the same job description as when you started. For example, some people who began their careers providing direct care to patients will move to more diverse opportunities; these might include work in administration, research, education, or even marketing and sales. Some will choose freely to change their roles, while others will be "encouraged" or mandated by their employers to change. Additionally, some health professionals who begin as employees will turn to self-employment and entrepreneurship, and still others will move from careers in private practice to work with an organization. As always, the future is both unknown and potentially very exciting.

As the options for work in health care change, the definitions of career success are also changing. Whereas success was once defined by others and typically involved an increase in rank, prestige, and pay, success is now often defined by the individual. To the new generation of professionals, success relates more to whether work is congruent with values, has meaning and impact, and supports a life that is balanced between home and work. Today, success at work is about being in control of your career and about making choices that fit with your vision of your future.

Many factors influence a professional's ability to benefit from opportunities and to grow with change rather than to merely react to it. While most of us know that we need to take control of our working lives and futures if we are going to make the most of new opportunities, we often do not know where to begin. Career planning is a strategy that can offer health professionals the means to respond to both short- and long-term changes in their profession and in the health care system as a whole. Planning and developing your career should be an essential part of your ongoing professional development. A process that includes continual assessment and goal setting, career planning is most successful when it is integrated into your everyday life, both personally and professionally. Luckily, as a health professional you are well positioned to begin planning your career because the skills you will need are the same ones you already use for problem solving, case management, and client care in your daily practice. Just as you learned to develop plans for your patients and clients, you must learn to design career plans for yourself—the skills you rely on are the same, but the focus or target is different. Career planning is directed inward—toward helping *you* achieve *your* goals.

How to Use This Handbook

This handbook addresses the need of all health professionals to take control of their careers, whether they are employees or self-employed, managers or front-line workers. Planning your working future is a process that can help you achieve professional and personal satisfaction at any stage of your career. Thinking about the ideas presented in this handbook will help you to understand why career planning is vital and will equip you with the knowledge and skills to make career planning a part of your ongoing professional development.

For over 15 years we have been working with health care providers, employers, and policymakers in the area of career planning and development. At the individual level, a wide range of health professionals have participated in our workshops and accessed our career coaching programs, both on-site and online in Canada, the United States, Europe, and South Africa. At the institutional level, we have worked in partnership with organizations to ensure that appropriate policies and infrastructure are in place to support individual health professionals. We have helped these organizations to develop a career-sensitive culture that contributes to a healthy workplace with healthy and satisfied staff.

When working with individuals we learned that, while our colleagues have dreams, goals, and ideas about their futures, they need and want help to take charge of their careers and learn how to integrate career planning into their ongoing professional and personal development. The people we have helped need a process to guide them in achieving the futures they want. After both editions of our first book on career planning, written for nurses, generated a great deal of interest, large numbers of other health professionals asked why they did not have a similar resource. In response to their wishes, we developed this handbook to guide all health professionals in applying career planning insights and skills toward meeting their professional needs.

Part Two of this handbook provides you with the context in which to begin your planning—a perspective on the world of health care and of health care work. In Part Three, we discuss the nature of your career as a continuum and explore the issues facing you at different stages of your work in health care. In Part Four, we introduce the Donner–Wheeler Career Planning and Development Model, which forms the foundation of the work we do. This model will provide you with a framework to guide you on your career journey. To help you apply the model, we have provided a number of exercises and questions you can complete as you develop your own customized career plan. This is a handbook—it is meant to be adaptable to your style and needs, so use it in the way that helps you most. Furthermore, go back to rethink and redo the exercises regularly.

This handbook will give you the tools to transform what you have been thinking and dreaming about into reality; it is not a quick fix or a recipe book, but an approach to helping you live a rewarding and autonomous professional life. We have written this book for those of you who are beginning your careers, for the large group of you now in mid-career, and for those of you planning retirement. Additionally, we have written this for those of you who want to continue to work in organizations, but also for those who want to be independent practitioners. Whether you love what you do and want to continue to do it or would like to move in a new direction, this handbook is for you. What we have written here encourages you to develop your skills in planning and developing your career— that is, it combines the *what* with the *how*. We hope this handbook helps you to think about your career in health care. Also, we hope it provides you with opportunities to take control, to plan, and to make some decisions about your future.

Part Two

Key Issues in the Current
Health Care Environment

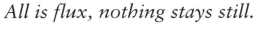

All is flux, nothing stays still.

Heraclitus

O ur world seems a smaller place today, as access to information about it is readily at hand. Moreover, health concerns and trends on a global scale often manifest themselves in issues that are national and even local. The gap between rich and poor, human resource shortages, and issues of war, disease, and safety are concerns for every region, and the issues are changing daily. Health care is a "moving target," and that is precisely why being able to control your own future is critical. The challenges facing providers and consumers in this first part of the twenty-first century are numerous, and the demand for services is like a proverbial "bottomless pit." In this context, it is vital to incorporate career planning into your professional development so that you can meet the challenges posed by this increasing demand and take advantage of all the exhilarating opportunities that they also afford. When confronting complex issues, you as a health professional must feel competent when navigating through the system in relation to your career; this includes knowing what you need and want before you make your choices. Furthermore, understanding the issues in your environment will provide you with key information needed to implement plans that ensure your skills, abilities, interests, and values find their place in the health care system. Thus, it is up to you, as a professional, to take responsibility for keeping as informed as possible about the broader issues that will affect your role, as well as taking responsibility for the well-being of your patients and your society.

The next section provides a snapshot of seven key issues that health care will face in the first few decades of the twenty-first century. Depending on where you live and what you do, the personal significance of each issue we present will vary; however, this overview will help you plan your own future by providing a broad context of what you will face. What follows is clearly not an exhaustive list, including all important issues of the day; it is meant to be taken as a guide to understanding the world in which you live and work. Later, we will ask you to consider some of the other issues that are relevant in your world.

Health Human Resources

The current shortage of all health professionals across the world is reaching near-crisis proportions, and the situation is projected to get worse. In both developed countries and those that are still developing, these shortages threaten the health and well-being of consumers and health care providers. "Working short" has become a common practice around the globe and has increased the stress and rate of illness for health providers, while decreasing morale. This practice has also caused stress for employers and health care organizations, leading to enormous challenges related to maintaining quality care in a safe environment. While work shortages can provide many opportunities for professionals, they can also make retaining those professionals problematic. This is the paradox: Where retention is poor, recruitment becomes even more difficult.

The challenges related to ensuring stable and productive human resources in health care have been identified in many reports and commissions, both Canadian and otherwise. Aging workforces, an increased demand for home care services, globalization, rapidly changing technology, and cultural diversity, as well as diversity between generations, all create obstacles and exacerbate the challenges already faced by human resource planners and policymakers. These individuals must work to recruit providers in general, and also to ensure that there is staff available to replace managers and leaders who are ready to retire; thus, succession planning has become a major part of the recruitment and retention challenge. It is clear that systematic and coordinated health human resource planning is needed in Canada and around the globe, and that these plans should focus on keeping recruited employees in their current professions and workplaces. Initiatives of this type are not only thought to be good for health care providers, but also for patients in that they improve safety and quality of care.

Technological Advances

Just as human resources present a current and future concern for health care, so does technological advancement. Having the appropriate technology available to provide care and helping providers learn to use it is very important. Technological advances are changing the way we practise. The skills we now need to do our jobs in health care have changed, which, in the future, may even change the kinds of people we need to recruit. Furthermore, the cost of technology will likely affect the kind of health care we can provide. Many illnesses are being treated today that, at one time, could not even be diagnosed, and great progress has been made in areas such as organ transplantation and microscopic surgery. However, the technology required to support these advances is expensive, and it has created a pyramid effect that has dramatically affected overall health care costs. Advanced treatments such as the ones mentioned have created a paradox for health care officials who must constantly weigh the interests of the consumer against the cost of providing care. Computers and hand-held devices have also both aided and complicated work in the health professions. On one hand, they have made access to information easier for providers and consumers, have made it easier to coordinate care, and have reduced duplication of diagnosis and treatment. At the same time, however, they have caused concerns about privacy and confidentiality. It is clear that the opportunities technology has provided for improving care and patient outcomes have also led to many challenges.

Chronic Illness and Health Care in the Community

In the developed world, an emphasis on community health has been slow to emerge because the focus of health care has been primarily hospital-based. Community health programs have tended to focus on preventive care and health promotion. Instead of remaining in the community, those with chronic illnesses have been cared for in institutions focused on custodial care rather than rehabilitation. In the past, very few patients were discharged from hospitals if they still required specialized care. Now, because lengths of stay in hospital have shortened, and because demographics are changing and consumers are better educated and more demanding, the place of care is also changing. Individuals with acute care needs as well as those with chronic diseases are being cared for in their own homes, where they expect the care to be as safe and as advanced as if they were in hospital. Integration and coordination of care become even more important as community- and home-based care increase. In this changing care environment, health professionals are increasingly finding opportunities for collaborative work in a wide variety of settings, and educational institutions and policymakers are running hard to keep up with the required changes.

Focus on Safety

An emphasis on quality assurance has given way to one on quality improvement, which is now heavily focused on patient safety. Since an Institute of Medicine report (Cohn, Corrigan, & Donaldson, 1999) documented the implications of medical error on mortality and morbidity in the United States, many other jurisdictions have made patient safety a top priority. This change in focus has created new roles for some health professionals, has led to a renewed emphasis on basic skills such as communication, and has increased attention to information technology as a means of improving quality and reducing error. This focus on patient safety has also created new opportunities for health professionals as the demand for expertise in the area continues to grow.

Multi-Generational Diversity

The issue of diversity between generations is worthy of special attention because it is critical to ensuring that we make the best use of the professionals we have in the health care workforce today. The differing values and priorities between professionals in the 50-plus age group and their younger colleagues must be addressed if we want to retain all of them in the workforce (Families and Work Institute, 2004, p. 8). One pressure point centres on the fact that the younger generation has grown up with technology and may be frustrated with its uneven use in health care, while the older group struggles daily to use and adapt to the new technologies. A second and perhaps more pressing division between these cohorts is the focus on work–life balance and attention to family that seems to dominate the younger generation's values. This particular focus often conflicts with the work-centred values of older professionals and can be the cause of tension and poor communication (Spinks & Moore, 2007). If we are unable to find ways to address the needs of younger workers, we will lose them. Additionally, if we do not develop policies and processes to help these two much-needed groups work together, our much-valued older workers will choose to leave health care just when we need them and their experience and institutional memory most.

Interprofessional Education and Practice

The value of teamwork and interprofessional practice is not a new idea. However, it is the subject of a newly energized focus that rewards professionals who can work with others in interprofessional teams to enhance patient care and improve safety and quality. The validated connection that has been made between interprofessional teamwork and quality care has resulted in increased attention to the matter by educators, policymakers, and administrators (D'Amour & Oandasan, 2005; Health Force Ontario, 2007, p. 11). Education, although still provided primarily in disciplinary silos, is starting to change. Courses and clinical experience now articulate the expectation that students will understand other health care disciplines, their priorities, and their practices, and that, furthermore, they will know how to work with others in the interests of the patient. We are in a phase of "one step forward and one back" in the area of interprofessional education and practice. There are many incentives to move forward, mostly related to the opportunities for improving patient care, but of course the reluctance of the discipline to "give anything up" also plays a role. These changes also create challenges for employers who are anxious to recruit and retain these "new" professionals in order to ensure their organization is moving forward on the twenty-first-century agenda. Regardless of the struggles involved, interprofessional collaboration, once a "nice-to-have," will soon be a "must-have."

Professional Responsibility

Self-regulation and its focus on accountability is a fundamental principle that differentiates professions from other occupations. In health care, we have seen an increasing focus on holding professionals accountable for their decisions and their work. As you think about and begin to plan your future, you need to consider the limits and opportunities that your scope of practice currently provides, and then think about what training and education you may require in order to expand your scope or change your role and practice. Continuous learning to ensure your competence is a professional responsibility. Many issues that surface in the workplace concerning employee-versus-employer responsibility are related to continual learning opportunities. Whose responsibility is it to provide, fund, and otherwise support continuing professional education? In self-regulating professions it is obviously the professionals who are accountable for their practice and their learning; however, employers certainly have a role to play in supporting their staff and colleagues. The provision of professional development opportunities is, in itself, a recruitment and retention strategy.

References

Cohn, L.T., Corrigan, J.J., & Donaldson, M.S. (Eds.). (1999). *To err is human: Building a safer health system.* Washington, DC: National Academic Press.

D'Amour, D., & Oandasan, I. (2005). Interprofessionality as the field of interprofessional practice and interprofessional education: An emerging concept. *Journal of Interprofessional Care, 19*(Suppl. I), 8–20.

Families and Work Institute. (2004), p. 8. *Older employees in the workforce: A companion brief to generation and gender in the workplace.* Retrieved August 28, 2008, from http://familiesandwork.org/site/research/reports/olderworkers.pdf

Health Force Ontario. (2007), p. 11. *Interprofessional care: A blueprint for action in Ontario.* Retrieved February 5, 2008, from www.healthforceontario.ca/upload/en/whatishfo/ipc%20blueprint%20final.pdf

Spinks, N., & Moore, C. (2007). The changing workforce, workplace and nature of work: Implications for health human resource management. *Canadian Journal of Nursing Leadership, 20*(3), 26–41.

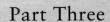
Part Three

Planning Throughout the Major Stages of Your Career

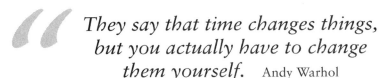

> *They say that time changes things, but you actually have to change them yourself.* Andy Warhol

The Career Continuum

Health care careers can generally be described as being comprised of five stages (adapted from Donner, 1992). In Stage One, *learning*, neophytes are introduced to their chosen profession. This phase occurs within a professional education or training program, where students are primarily concerned with learning to "become" health professionals and how to do the work of that profession.

The Career Continuum

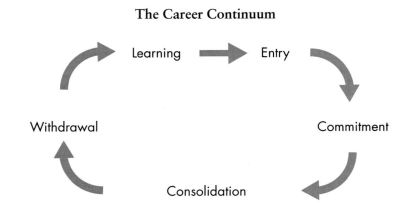

Stage Two, *entry*, begins when newly graduated professionals select their first workplace. This is the time when new graduates explore their options and begin to think about areas of practice that could be both rewarding and appropriate to their interests and skills. Depending on the profession, this period might be a long one involving years of residency and fellowship, or it may be somewhat shorter and involve experimenting with different positions and work environments.

During *commitment*, Stage Three, professionals identify their likes and dislikes in terms of clinical areas, geography, workplace climate, and other factors that may vary from job to job. This is when professionals typically evaluate career goals, seek mentors, consider continuing their education or refocusing their practice, and generally seek to find the right "fit" between themselves and their work setting.

Stage Four, *consolidation*, finds professionals comfortable with their chosen career path and with the relationship between their personal and professional lives. This fourth stage is notable for a professional's dedication to career and commitment to continuous learning, and for their focus on making a contribution to health care and society. In this stage, health professionals begin to mentor and coach others, and to assume leadership roles in professional and community organizations. Usually, "consolidation" is the longest stage in a career, but it is certainly not a static one; this stage is typically characterized by variety in terms of roles, tasks, and responsibilities. In Stage Five, *withdrawal*, professionals begin to think about what comes next, and prepare to either retire, or to move on to a new career.

Recognizing Opportunities and Challenges During Major Periods of a Health Career

As you move along the career continuum, your skills develop, your needs change, and your goals and plans evolve. Career planning is thus both important and useful at every stage of your career; it is a dynamic process that adapts to changes in you and in the world in which you live and work. For the purposes of career planning, it may be easiest to think of yourself as being in the early, mid, or late period of your professional career so that you can consider how the issues relevant to your stage of the continuum affect you. These three career periods are associated with particular opportunities and vulnerabilities for you, your profession, and your employer or organization.

The Early-Career Professional

Beginning to work in health care is tough, but it is also exciting. You have worked hard over the course of your academic career, and you have developed the skills, knowledge, and professional attitude required for professional practice. While you are ready to work in a variety of settings, choosing the right one can be a big challenge. For some, this early period feels very vulnerable; you may worry that you have made the wrong choice and should not be a health professional at all, or you may be concerned that you will never find the right environment to suit your lifestyle and values. You may also be grappling with a number of life challenges at this time that can include dealing with separation from friends and family as you move on from your academic institution, forming intimate and perhaps lasting relationships, and managing financial issues such as student loan repayment. At the same time, you are finding your way in your new profession and learning how to articulate what you need from your workplace. For example, during this period you might determine that management is an area you would like to pursue and begin to embark on studies to help you reach that goal.

Here are some of the questions you will need to consider during the early part of your career:

- What is my knowledge and what are my skills?
- Where do I need help?
- What kind of environment will enable me to grow and develop in my profession?
- What network of colleagues, mentors, and supervisors do I need and want?
- Where do I see myself in the next five years, and how will what I am doing now help me get there?

The answers you generate from these questions will help you make the most of your beginner status and ensure that you move forward positively.

The definition of "beginner" is a difficult one, and it is perhaps best defined by the professional him- or herself. Some of us take five or more years of working to feel that we are doing what we want to be doing and doing it in the right place, while others feel "right" within the first couple of years. It is important for both the professional and the employer (where the professional is employed) to understand that individual aptitudes and working styles play a role in determining where one is on the career continuum.

It is worth noting that the early period in a professional's career is also an important stage for one's profession and employer. If beginners cannot take their places in the professional world by finding work environments that fit with their goals and values, they may choose to leave their jobs, and perhaps even their professions. Therefore, it is imperative that mature colleagues, professional organizations, and planners of health care settings be purposeful in the policies and practices that they implement for beginners.

The Mid-Career Professional

Whether a person is "mid-career" has little to do with age or the number of years spent on a given career path, and more to do with being at a crossroads. Once you have been in the consolidation stage of your career for some time, where you have become comfortable with your chosen career, achieved some goals, and negotiated the relationship between your personal and professional lives, you have likely reached a point at which you are vulnerable to restlessness. While you have now pursued your education, developed your practice, cared for your family, and given significant energy and a number of years to the health care system, you may now be questioning your future in health care, and asking yourself these questions: "What have my life and career been 'about'?" "What is my purpose?," and "What is the legacy I want to leave?"

The questions above, and their answers, are particularly important to your profession and clients because neither can afford to lose you. Currently, mid-career professionals are the largest cohort in health care; however, they have the professional memory that the system counts on, the expertise that patients and clients require, and the experience and wisdom that younger professionals depend on. Therefore, many jurisdictions are recognizing the need to retain their mid-career professionals. Retention strategies that provide mid-career professionals with opportunities to refresh and renew themselves are critical to ensure quality care and patient safety.

Now at mid-career, you have acquired numerous transferable skills that you can take outside of health care. At this point, if options do not seem available to you in your workplace and you cannot see opportunities for further development within your profession, or if you can no longer see the significance of your work in your life, you are at risk of becoming complacent or bitter. You may even decide to leave your profession for these reasons. However, it is clear that mid-career is the period in which there is significant opportunity for change and renewal. Still, taking the time to focus on yourself is an opportunity that most of us do not seize often enough. You should answer these three questions for yourself at this time:

- Where have I been?
- Where am I now?
- Where would I like to go?

The process of re-evaluating your past and future involves a bit of the angst you may have felt during the early days of your career, but the process should be simpler now that you have more skills, expertise, and experience. In other words, you have more options. Mid-career is also a time when balancing home and work may assume more significance for professionals. Career-related decisions are often influenced by choices around the kind of life one wants to lead and the other responsibilities within that life, as well as interests in leisure or other activities. This is the time when you must decide what you want and what is possible.

In 1993, Beverly Kaye coined the phrase "up is not the only way" in her book of the same name, and argued for a shift from defining career success vertically to a new, multidirectional model—that is, from a ladder to a lattice. In mid-career you can choose from several career directions: lateral (moving sideways), vertical (moving up), or realignment (moving down or out). In a lateral move, you seek out a new position but stay at the same level of responsibility. Moving laterally is not only a great way to increase your knowledge and experience, but also to recharge your batteries through renewed job satisfaction. Alternatively, although "up is not the only way," it may be the way you choose to go. While the flatter organizational structures now favoured by health care institutions have resulted in fewer formal leadership positions, there are always some opportunities for a vertical move within an organization.

Many of us are looking for a better work–life balance, either because we have multiple demands, or because we would like to work less as we age. Realignment or moving down—that is, taking a role with less responsibility—can help you achieve that balance. Instead, you may choose to leave your current role or workplace and adopt a job with fewer demands. Or, of course, you can always choose to stay right where you are, to grow and develop in place.

The Late-Career Professional

The late-career period is challenging in several ways, as you think about what it means to be an older adult. This can be a stressful time as you consider how aging is affecting your interest in practising your profession, and even your competence. Also, you are likely focusing on your priorities and available options. However, this can also be a very rewarding time because you now have permission to review your contributions to the well-being of your patients or clients, your organization, and your field. Also, you now have permission to consider new options that, previously, you may have only dreamed about. Late in your career you will need to decide if and when you want to retire, and then you will need to plan for retirement or to move to a new opportunity. Therefore, the developmental tasks of this period involve determining how you will spend the last years or months of your present career and preparing for what you will do afterward.

Late-career is not an end; it is a new beginning, and it is up to you to determine what it will look like. Will this time be devoted to leisure, to another career opportunity, to community involvement, or to a combination of all of these things? Today, there seem to be as many definitions for retirement as there are people retiring. Whereas retirement used to mean travelling, playing golf, and maybe volunteering a little bit, today it may also involve taking on another career, working part-time, or becoming an entrepreneur or "dollar-a-year" executive. To complicate matters further, as you contemplate retiring, you may feel pressure not to leave as managers and health care organizations struggle to find replacements for large numbers of retiring professionals.

The concept of "retirement" thus no longer comes with an automatic plan—it is something that each of us must define and construct for ourselves. Just as career planning is so much more than finding and keeping a job, retirement planning involves much more than ensuring you will have the necessary financial resources to stop working. Many of us spend a good part of our careers talking about what we will do "when we retire," and yet few of us are really ready for retirement. We may have done the financial planning, determined where we will live, and planned for some extended vacations, but rarely have we actually talked to ourselves and others about what retirement means to us and what we are hoping to get out of it—that is, what our visions and goals are. Also, it is very easy to get caught up in the definitions and expectations of family, friends, and colleagues for what our own retirements should look like. These issues come to the surface as we move from being fully engaged in our careers to looking for opportunities that are less stressful, both physically and emotionally. Therefore, we need to think of retirement as a part of our careers rather than an afterthought—as a new chapter in our lives.

If we view our careers in a holistic way, then retirement is not a new event, but rather a part of our career continuum. Who we are, what we value, and what we like do not change because we retire; these things are just lived out in different ways. If we want our retirements to feel successful, then we need to consider them in the same ways that we consider the other phases of our careers.

Retirement can be an exciting phase of your life, career-wise, and one that lets you fit your strengths and interests to opportunities out there in the greater world. What happens in your retirement, just like what happens during the rest of your career, can be up to you, but you need to take charge of this time. Regardless of when you begin thinking about retirement, what is important is that you think about it in an organized and systematic way. To help you get started, here are a few questions:

- What does retirement mean to me?
- Am I ready to retire?
- What pleasures and benefits do I get from my work?
- What are my priorities?
- What is my desired financial picture for the future?

Late-career is not only a time for retirement planning. You may plan to stay employed but be considering how to manage some of the effects of healthy aging, or even learning how to deal with chronic illness while continuing to work. This is where some of the options we discussed for the mid-career period may be relevant again. Moving laterally, down, or out, or realigning yourself within your organization may all help you continue to be active professionally while maintaining your health.

Where Do I Go From Here?

We have provided you with a lot to think about as you consider your career and how you would like to be in this world. All of this material is intended to function as the context from which you can begin to do some serious work planning your career future. In Part Four of this handbook, we introduce the Donner–Wheeler Career Planning and Development Model, along with a variety of practical tools and exercises. You can use these to apply the framework learned in Parts One to Three in order to start planning your own career and the rest of your life. Let the work begin!

References

Donner, G.J. (1992). Career development and mobility issues. In A. Baumgart & J. Larsen (Eds.), *Canadian nursing faces the future* (2nd ed., 345–363). St. Louis, MO: Mosby Year Book.

Kaye, B. (1993). *Up is not the only way: A guide to developing workforce talent.* Washington, DC: Career Systems.

Part Four

Using the Donner–Wheeler Model to Plan Your Career

P art Four is organized specifically around the five-phase Donner–Wheeler Career Planning and Development Model to give you a process to use as you move from recognizing career possibilities to taking action. The model is a focused professional development strategy that will help you take greater ownership of your career and help you to prepare for ever-changing workplace environments. The planning process taught by the Donner–Wheeler Model is iterative and continuous; as you use it, you will move back and forth between phases with a goal always in sight, rather than moving in a lockstep linear way. The model requires you to:

- understand the environment in which you live and work,
- assess your strengths and limitations and then validate your assessment,

- articulate your personal career vision,
- develop a realistic plan for the future, and
- market yourself to achieve your career goals.

The Donner–Wheeler Career Planning and Development Model

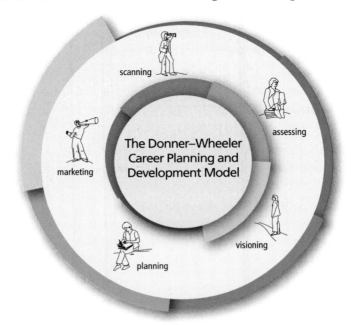

In each phase of Part Four you will learn about a part of the Donner–Wheeler Model—you will learn what it is, why it is important, and how to apply it to your own career planning. Then, you will have an opportunity to complete a number of activities that relate to the phase you have studied. The benefit you will glean from Part Four will be in direct proportion to the effort and time you put into completing the activities.

You should move through Part Four in the way that best suits your learning style—this is very important. However, here is a suggested method to help you get the most out of this experience:

Read the description of each phase, then the questions that relate to that phase. Think about each question and its relevance to you and your career. Then, either answer the questions at the end of each section or proceed to the end and answer them all at once. Answer them as honestly as you can, keeping in mind that the answers are for your eyes alone. Do not be overwhelmed by the number of questions; they are offered only as a catalyst to get you thinking. Pace yourself, set a schedule, and keep to it. Finally, if you need help sticking to your schedule, consider working through the questions with a colleague, a group of friends, or a coach, either face-to-face or virtually.

> *"What you get by reaching your destination is not nearly as important as what you will become by reaching your destination."*
> Zig Ziglar

Before you begin to plan where you want to go, it is helpful to know where you are. We have developed a "Career Readiness Checklist" to help you do a quick assessment of how much you already know about the career planning process and how much you have done. Read each item and put a check mark beside the ones that apply to you.

CAREER READINESS Checklist

Scanning

☐ I am aware of the current realities and future trends within health care and my profession at the local, national, and global levels.

☐ I am aware of the local, national, and global realities and future trends outside health care and my profession that can impact the way I work and how the health care industry works.

Assessing

☐ I can articulate my values as they relate to my career.

☐ I can describe my strengths and how I use them in my work.

☐ I can describe my limitations.

☐ I know how others would describe me.

☐ I can describe three significant accomplishments I have made in the past three to five years.

☐ My current position is a good match with my values, beliefs, knowledge, skills, and interests.

☐ I make time to do the things that are important to me in my personal life.

Visioning

☐ I can describe my ideal vision or visions for my work.

Planning

☐ I can identify career goals that are related to my vision.

☐ I have a written career development plan in place.

☐ I know what steps to take over the next six to twelve months to further my career.

Marketing

☐ I have established a relevant network.

☐ I have, or am considering acquiring, a mentor or a coach.

☐ I continue to develop my communication skills through written and oral presentations.

☐ I have an up-to-date résumé.

How did you do? Are there some areas that you would like to improve upon? This baseline checklist will help you determine which of the phases you need to work hardest on and which might go a little more quickly. The checklist will also help you to assess what you have learned about career planning and development once you have completed the process. Therefore, it functions as a kind of pre- and post-test. Now you are ready to begin to learn and use the Donner–Wheeler Career Planning and Development Model.

PHASE ONE

Scanning Your Environment

 *It was the best of times,
it was the worst of times.*

Charles Dickens

What Is Scanning?

Scanning your environment can be described as taking stock of the world in which you live and work. Doing this involves understanding the current realities and future trends in your industry at the local, national, and global levels. Scanning is a universal skill and can be applied to any sector. Part Two of this handbook contains an example of a scan of the health care environment.

Why Is Scanning Important?

Scanning is a continual activity that, together with self-assessment, forms the foundation of the career planning process. By scanning, we become better informed and learn to see the world from differing perspectives; also, we become able to identify current and future career opportunities, and to recognize the personal limitations that we will have to address in order to move forward. Reading, talking with others, continuing our educations, and otherwise exposing ourselves to information and ideas from inside and outside our chosen fields are some ways that we observe, learn about, and assess the world around us. When asked to think about the word *environment,* you should not only conjure up a close-up picture of the setting in which you practise, but also a wide-angle shot of the broader area that surrounds you—that is, the external conditions that you live within. Just as you would not consider providing care to a client without knowing something about the person's health status, family, and socio-economic circumstances, before planning your career you must think about the broader context of your surroundings and how current trends and future developments in health care could affect your working future. Scanning is the easiest and most productive way to place yourself as an observer, rather than a player, in the world in which you live. It permits you to see beyond your immediate circumstances to grasp what is possible, to think about new things in new ways, and to open yourself to opportunities without censoring any of your ideas. If we are to understand what is happening now and what may be happening in the future, each of us must scan continually and in a variety of ways throughout our careers.

"The true journey of discovery does not consist in searching for new territories, but in having new eyes."

Marcel Proust

How to Do a Scan

When was the last time you stopped what you were doing, paused, and looked around? What did you observe? Often, we get so caught up in our own world of work that we fail to recognize the issues and trends that will have a direct impact on us. Reading, talking, and listening, both face-to-face and virtually—skills that health professionals have as part of their repertoire of behaviours—are the means we use to make sense of all of the information we collect. Scanning is not a task to be completed on a schedule; rather, it should be an integral part of everyday professional and personal life.

When you do your own scan, you should not only consider the health care environment, but also the social, political, and economic environments in which you live. While these environments affect the practice of health care, they also often influence the range of career opportunities available to health professionals. Professional and popular journals, conversations with friends and colleagues, everyday experiences and observations, and the Internet are all good sources of information about the external world.

Think of your scan as written in pencil, not ink, and as something you continually update to reflect the changing environment; if you are prepared in that way, you should be able to identify local, national, and global trends and issues at any given time. You can then use your scan to help position yourself and your career in the future.

ACTIVITY 1   Scanning Your Environment

Before you begin your first independent scan, do the following:
Refer back to Part Two (pages 7–14), where we provided you with an overview scan of several key trends and issues in health care. Because that scan represents one point in time, is there anything you can add now? Jot it down.

_____

_____

_____

_____

_____

_____

Next, save your local newspapers for a week, or go online for news. Highlight all of the stories that could have an impact on your practice, your profession, or the health care system. How many did you find? Were you surprised by the number or types of items that you circled? What else surprised you? What did not surprise you? Finally, do you view the stories you found differently from a provider's and a user's perspective?

_____

_____

_____

_____

_____

_____

It is now time to try to do a scan on your own. The same approach to looking at trends, issues, and priorities that is described above can be used to examine your place of work, your community, or your profession. Choose one area to focus on; what are three current issues, priorities, or trends facing the area you chose? Write down what you have found.

_____

_____

_____

_____

_____

_____

What Have You Accomplished?

The trends and issues you have identified in your scan will serve as a basis for you to make informed decisions about career options, helping you plan to strategically explore them. Thinking about the issues and trends that you have identified in your environment, consider which ones are specifically meaningful for you, and highlight them. Remember that you will need to review and update your scan on a regular basis to change or expand the initial number of items and to re-evaluate their relevance to you.

Now list three things that you have learned from Phase One:

1. _____

2. _____

3. _____

Did anything surprise you? How? Why?

_____

_____

_____

_____

_____

Identify one thing you currently do that will be influenced by what you have learned from your scan.

_____

_____

_____

_____

_____

What is one thing that you would like to follow up on or learn more about?

_____

_____

_____

_____

_____

_____

What Is Your Next Step?

If you had difficulty answering some of the questions, then your next step is to connect with others who can assist you, for example, colleagues, leaders, family, and friends. If you have enough data to move on, your next step is to turn your sights inward and answer the question "Who am I?" In Phase Two, *Completing Your Self-Assessment,* you will get a sense of how your interests, values, and abilities can fit with where society and the world of health care are heading.

assessing

PHASE TWO

Completing Your Self-Assessment

> *Real value can only be given by people who know their own value. How can any of us know our true value if we never take inventory?* John Scherer

What Is Assessing?

Now that you have scanned your environment and learned what surrounds you, and now understand how those things might be relevant for you and your career, it is time to turn the focus on yourself. A self-assessment enables you to identify your values, experiences, knowledge, strengths, and limitations; it also includes a reality check, a process through which you solicit feedback from others to validate what you have identified. Once you complete your self-assessment, you integrate it with your environmental scan; this creates your career vision and helps you identify the direction to take as you plan your future. As you begin your self-assessment, you will first identify all the attributes that make you who you are and that define what you have to offer to the health care environment. Completing Phase Two allows you to give honest and accurate answers to two questions: "Who am I?" and "How am I seen by others?"

Why Is Assessing Important?

Whether the job market is tight or opportunities are plentiful, you must be able to recognize your attributes and take the initiative to market your skills to others, including prospective employers, colleagues, and members of your community. To market yourself you need to be able to articulate your accomplishments clearly and persuasively so that they reveal your values, skills, and interests. Self-assessment will help you do this; it will also help you recognize which opportunities or jobs you will best fit with and be most successful pursuing. This is what completing a self-assessment does— it involves giving yourself the time and permission to concentrate on looking inward, and to take stock and then develop a personal and professional profile. Self-assessment requires reflection, the ability to ask yourself some hard questions, and the determination to validate your responses with others. Additionally, it must become an ongoing process in your continuous professional and personal learning and development.

Over the years, you have likely come to understand what you like or dislike doing and have acquired some sense of your strengths and limitations. You may also have developed skills and expertise outside of your profession. Who you are now may be very different from who you were when you first chose your career. However, without a deliberate and systematic self-assessment you can, at best, have only a limited picture of who you really are. How, then, can you know what you want and what you are capable of doing now, let alone how to take control and direct your future? If you neglect the self-assessment phase in the career planning and development process, you will be driven only by the needs of the market or the opinions of others when you start to make decisions.

Although completing a self-assessment takes time, the result is an increased awareness of your strengths and limitations. The assessment process will also help you learn about which facets of yourself have remained untapped or unexpressed, and how you can develop those things. Moreover, you will begin to understand how you may be limited by learned perceptions, familiar but unsatisfying roles, or others' expectations. Then, you will be better able to capitalize on your strengths and life experiences.

> *"If life is to have meaning, the extent to which you know yourself is the most important work you will ever do."*
> Gregory Crow

How to Do a Self-Assessment

As you begin your self-assessment, think of all the attributes that make you who you are and define what you have to offer to society. Completing your self-assessment allows you to give honest and accurate answers to the question "Who am I?" The sooner you begin a systematic process of self-assessment—whether you are a new recruit, an experienced practitioner, or someone contemplating retirement—the more relevant and meaningful the results will be, leading to a good match between you and the work you do.

It is important to make sure that your self-assessment is comprehensive. Start by thinking about who you are from a number of perspectives. How would you describe your personality, your attitude, how you work with others, and your comfort with communication? For example, would you describe yourself as outgoing or quiet? Do you prefer to work alone or in groups? Can you easily communicate your points to your clients and other professionals? Self-assessment is as much about your personal qualities and special interests as it is about your professional knowledge and clinical skills. A broad range of skills is highly desirable now in the health care field. Therefore, the more comprehensive you can be about who you are—as a person and as a professional—the easier it will be to market yourself when the time comes.

Work is just one part of our lives, and for this reason, answering the question "Who am I?" involves much more than stating your job title or describing what you do. Even though we spend a considerable amount of time on our work, we cannot ignore the other things that make our lives feel complete, including our families, friends, health, financial resources, and the communities we live in. As you move through your self-assessment, you need to keep the whole "you" in mind. We are all unique, and the challenge lies in being able to articulate that uniqueness. This is what a self-assessment helps you to do—to answer the question "What makes me unique?"

Completing a self-assessment to discover who you are is like looking at a tapestry—rich in the colours and designs that reflect all of you. It will show you where you have been and where you are now, both personally and professionally. Just as your self continues to unfold through the course of your life, so, too, must self-assessment be a continuous part of your development, as you are influenced by new experiences throughout your career. A self-assessment includes an examination of values, knowledge, skills, interests, and accomplishments. Let us begin with values.

Assessing Your Values

Our values are those principles we prize, cherish, or esteem—the beliefs we consider to be most important. Cooperation, teamwork, family and friends, financial prudence, prestige, growth, and intellectual challenge are some common values that may direct our decisions and bring meaning to our lives. Psychologists suggest that ultimate satisfaction comes from living and working in concert with our values. What you value can provide insight into what you will be likely to champion, defend, and act upon in the future.

However, values are not static; they change and evolve over time, and so it is important to re-examine them routinely. Avoid making decisions based on what was once important to you, and frequently ask yourself, "Is there still congruence between my values and my employer's? Is there still congruence between my values and my personal relationships?" As you begin your self-assessment, identify those of your values that are present in your current role and those that are not. For example, if you are at a stage in your personal life where family is important, you should think about whether your employer shares these values because this will affect your happiness in your job and, therefore, your decision whether to stay in the position. Similarly, if the opportunity to learn is important to you, a workplace that offers a means of continuing your education, either formally or informally, will be of greater value to you.

Assessing Your Knowledge and Skills

Knowledge is developed through a combination of learning and experience. As you consider the knowledge you have acquired, you will benefit from reviewing both your past education (including the degrees, diplomas, and specialty certificates you have acquired) and the more recent workshops and seminars you have attended. What is your area of expertise? How has that expertise been developed through your work experience?

Skills, on the other hand, are developed or acquired abilities. There are two general categories of skills: "hard skills," or technical abilities most commonly acquired through education or training; and "soft skills," such as communication, coordination, support, and adaptability. Soft skills are typically acquired through a combination of education and life experience. They are often highly transferable, meaning that they can be applied to a broad range of settings and situations. Gaps or limitations in both hard and soft skills are as important to acknowledge as your strengths. If you do not recognize your limitations and act to address them, you may assume roles for which you are ill-suited. This will only inhibit your happiness and your ability to succeed.

Interests can be grouped into four categories:

1. People: Activities may include helping, serving, and caring for others, or selling goods and services.

2. Data: People with this interest enjoy working with facts, records, or files.

3. Things: This interest involves working with machines, tools, or living things.

4. Ideas: Tasks include developing insights, theories, or new ways of expressing ideas, or of approaching a task.

Assessing Your Interests

It is also important to examine our interests as part of a self-assessment. Interests provide another measure of "fit" between our current work and what we would ideally like to be doing. Think about the work you have done so far, and the life you have lived. What has excited you and made you feel most alive and fulfilled? Once you determine these things, you can go about planning how to "chase" those feelings. For instance, if working with technology challenges and stimulates you, then working with an organization that is moving to an electronic filing system may be attractive. Alternatively, if you like constant change and do not need to establish continuing relationships with clients, clinical work in an emergency or urgent care facility could be an excellent career choice. When weighing your options, remember that your interests keep you happy and fulfilled over the long term. Therefore, finding work that matches your interests is just as important as being good at your job and securing a position that fits with your values.

Recognizing and Acknowledging Your Accomplishments

As you approach the completion of your self-assessment, you should be able to identify your strengths, limitations, and accomplishments from at least the past five, ten, or fifteen years. Remembering your accomplishments will be especially useful here in helping you to answer the question of who you are. An accomplishment is created when you go beyond what is expected; it cannot be listed in a job description. Rather, to have accomplished something means that you've identified a challenge, applied a specific approach, and had a successful outcome. Accomplishments do not need to be monumental as long as they represent the times in your life that you made a difference and felt proud of yourself for what you were able to achieve. An accomplishment can be anything from chairing the fundraising committee at your child's school to being chosen to represent your unit on a committee, or to having an article published. Your accomplishments reflect you at your personal or professional best.

ACTIVITY 2   Completing Your Self-Assessment

1. Values

To get started, list the top five values, principles, or character traits that matter most to you, ranking them in order of importance. These should be the factors that best define who you are at work and in your personal life.

1. _____

2. _____

3. _____

4. _____

5. _____

Now, using the chart below, focus on value #1. How well are you satisfying this value at work? In your personal life? If the answer to either question is high, that is great; if it is not, why? Are there any improvements you can make? Now that you have practised with value #1, go to value #2 and repeat the process.

VALUES

Value #1

On a scale of 1 to 5, with 5 being most congruent, how congruent is this value with my work?	On a scale of 1 to 5, how congruent is this value with my personal life?
1 2 3 4 5	1 2 3 4 5

How can I better support this value at work?

How can I better support this value in my personal life?

2. Knowledge and Skills

Think of the roles you have held that have been most important to your development. Consider not only the professional work you have done, but also the skills you have developed outside of your workplace, perhaps as a community volunteer or as a parent. What might help you to do this is to reflect on your role in projects that have yielded positive feedback. Now, finish the following three statements:

I am knowledgeable about:

_____

_____

_____

_____

_____

_____

These are my strengths:

(Planning and organizing, team building, and strategic thinking are some common strengths for health professionals.)

_____

_____

_____

_____

_____

_____

These are my limitations:

(These might include "not assertive," "limited knowledge," "not technologically savvy," or "poor problem solver.")

_____

_____

_____

_____

_____

_____

_____

3. Interests

As you consider the various roles you've played in your career, also think about the kinds of things that interest you; go beyond what your knowledge and skills are to consider what you enjoy doing.

What energizes or motivates me?

_____

_____

_____

_____

_____

_____

_____

What have I liked about my past jobs or roles?

_____

_____

_____

_____

_____

_____

What have I disliked about my past jobs or roles?

_____

_____

_____

_____

_____

What do I like about my current job or role?

_____

_____

_____

_____

_____

What do I not enjoy in my current job or role?

_____

_____

_____

_____

_____

In what type of environment do I perform at my best?

_____

_____

_____

_____

_____

What habits and styles of learning appeal to me?

_____

_____

_____

_____

_____

What types of people do I like to have around me?

_____

_____

_____

_____

_____

What do I like to do that is separate from my work?

_____

_____

_____

_____

_____

4. Accomplishments

Draw a line representing the last 10 years of your life and plot the points on that line that indicate the most significant highlights or milestones in your life so far. Remember, these accomplishments will be marked by the times that you felt most proud, alive, energized, committed, and fulfilled, and when you felt you "made a difference."

Now, take a look at what you've created; do you notice some common themes? Choose *one* of your accomplishments and use it to fill in the following table. What did it take for you to achieve that accomplishment? How does it fit with your values, knowledge, skills, and interests? If you were in the same situation again, is there anything you would have done differently?

ACCOMPLISHMENT

Accomplishment (note the situation, action, and result):

Which of my values were supported here?

What knowledge and skills did I use? Which did I acquire?

How interested was I in the project or initiative?

What did I learn from this experience?

Asking for Feedback: Doing a Reality Check

While asking for feedback is not easy, successful career planning depends on your being open to new ideas and perspectives. A reality check is simply the practice of seeking feedback on your strengths and limitations. By reflecting on others' perspectives, you are expanding the way you see yourself and answering the question "How do others see me?" A reality check involves listening to and accepting positive feedback, and also acknowledging the areas where change is needed. Seeking advice about what new skills you may require and how to develop them is also essential. You need a range of opinions to approximate an objective version of what is true.

Feedback can be instrumental to your career when it is delivered and received constructively. Moreover, it is most effective when communicated in the context of a supportive relationship that encourages growth and self-development. For instance, you may have an unrealistic view of your own expertise, which can lead to disappointment if you set your sights on a career goal that is beyond your skill set. Alternatively, you may have an inaccurately low opinion of your abilities; this may prevent you from seeking opportunities well within your reach, or lead you to "sell yourself short" in your current role. For these reasons, be prepared to invite feedback and to listen carefully to what you hear. Ask for input about how to develop new knowledge, skills, and abilities, and acknowledge those areas in yourself where change is needed.

How to Complete Your Reality Check

Careful career planning requires formal and informal feedback from colleagues, managers, friends, and family—people whose opinions you value. Often, individuals are hesitant to boast about what they have accomplished and how they have made a difference—it feels uncomfortable, and yet receiving feedback affirms where we shine.

Before others can give us feedback, they need to know that we are open to hearing what they have to say. Think of five people you could approach for feedback. Start with a couple of individuals whom you trust, and whose opinions you value; find an opportunity to meet with them. Then, consider seeking feedback from someone whom you know, but not as well, and ask the same questions. While this may be risky, the responses you hear from your acquaintances will enhance your self-assessment. There may be many resources to which you can turn to validate your self-assessment. A valuable one is the performance management program in your place of employment that may include goal-setting and also performance appraisal. The evaluation component of projects, committees, and other activities may also provide some valuable information for you, including notes of appreciation or personal notes that you may have taken when you received feedback in the past.

Asking for feedback after you have completed your self-assessment is a crucial step. Remember, you are asking others to enrich your self-assessment, not to do it for you. Be clear about what feedback you want—what do you want to ask, learn, or share? Go to your meeting prepared, with some specific questions in mind; also consider sending your questions in advance, so the person helping you will be prepared. Finally, remember to follow up with a thank-you call or note to acknowledge the other person's time and honesty.

ACTIVITY 3　Completing Your Reality Check

Look at the description of the accomplishment that you identified on page 51. Did anyone else know about this accomplishment? If the answer is yes, what feedback did you get?

_____

_____

_____

_____

_____

_____

What did others identify as your strengths and limitations with regard to this accomplishment? What suggestions for improvement did they make?

_____

_____

_____

_____

_____

_____

_____

What three adjectives would (or did) the person or people providing feedback use to describe you and why?

1. _____

2. _____

3. _____

If no one knew about this accomplishment—that is, if you received no feedback, why not?

_____

_____

_____

_____

_____

_____

_____

What Have You Accomplished?

Your life experiences, values, self-knowledge, and goals will change over time. In your career, not only will your experience be varied and include different opportunities, but your levels of expertise may broaden or become highly specialized. Additionally, over the years, you will develop in many ways outside of the professional arena. Personal interests change and grow, family commitments fluctuate, demanding more or less attention, and beliefs and values become clearer. Documenting your personal and professional history will provide you with an inventory of inner resources that will serve you well as you develop an ongoing career plan that will be realistic and fulfilling.

Success and satisfaction depend on having the courage, confidence, and will to be authentic in your work. Now that you have completed a self-assessment, you should be able to recognize and appreciate the full range of your inner resources: your intelligence, knowledge, skills, interests, personality, values, and motivations. With an accurate sense of who you are and how others see you, you will be ready to explore opportunities, and to determine where you will have the most to contribute. Regularly revisiting your self-assessment will allow you to update your knowledge of yourself, to set learning goals, to develop career aspirations and action plans, and to feel confident that you still love the work you do. An awareness of your personal resources is a form of capital that invests in your future—use it and you will be the one in charge of your own career, both now and in the future.

Now list three things that you have learned from Phase Two:

1. _____

2. _____

3. _____

Did anything surprise you? How? Why?

_____

_____

_____

_____

_____

_____

Identify one thing you currently do that will be influenced by what you have learned from your self-assessment.

_____

_____

_____

_____

_____

_____

What is one thing you have learned about yourself that you would like to follow up on?

_____

_____

_____

_____

_____

_____

What Is Your Next Step?

At this point, you may feel that you require additional professional assistance to complete a more formal and comprehensive self-assessment. In this case, your next step may be to explore some resources that will assist you with this stage of your process. Appendix A contains a list of resources that may be helpful.

When you have completed a thorough self-assessment, your confidence and self-esteem will soar. You will also be ready to navigate Phase Three, *Creating Your Career Vision,* and to answer the question "What, then, do I want to do?"

visioning

PHASE THREE

Creating Your Career Vision

> *Purpose is the spark;*
> *vision is the flame.*
>
> K. McCarthy

What Is Visioning?

"Vision" is another word for a dream, or an image of potentiality. Your career vision is the link between who you are and what you can become. Where do you see yourself going? Do you like what you are currently doing, feel it is a good fit with your personal life, and want to develop within that role? Or, have you learned that you enjoy change and variety, and that it may be time to move on to other challenges? Having a career vision is perhaps the most forceful motivator for change that an individual can possess. Those who have a career vision speak in terms of what is possible; they make use of all their resources and have the ability to harness and focus their energy. Once you have determined a realistic and comprehensive picture of your values, beliefs, skills, and interests and have assessed these things in the context of a real-world scan, you are ready to think about your career possibilities.

Why Is Visioning Important?

More often than not, we construct visions for our personal lives—the trip we dream about taking, the home we would like to purchase, or the hopes we hold for our family's future—and then set plans to ensure that these dreams are realized. Yet when it comes to our professional lives, we often resist dreaming about what could be possible for our careers. Our dreams sustain us and keep us moving forward; that is why individuals need to create visions that describe where they want to go in their professional lives, and then to develop action plans that will develop those dreams into realities. Our career visions will sustain us as the health care environment continues to evolve.

To shape your future, you must hold an image in your mind of what it is you really want. It is using your imagination in this way, whether initiated by idle dreaming or conscious intention, that will propel you into the future. Think back to when you chose your career. You likely formed some type of vision at this time of what your ideal future would look like in terms of work, and probably envisioned a life filled with meaning and significance, in which you had a purpose and a reason for being. We all need a purpose, an answer to the question "Why do I exist?" before formulating a projection into the future. Purpose is a permanent, common thread woven throughout all parts of our lives; it exists in the past, present, and future. What is your purpose in life?

Visioning is future-based; it inspires us because, through its deliberate nature, it paints a visual picture of where we are going. Visioning involves a directional question: "Where am I going with my purpose?" Over the years, you, your workplace, and the health care system have all undergone changes. Therefore, you should continually reassess whether your original vision is still valid, given your current reality. Ask yourself, "Am I still feeling the way I felt when I chose my career—am I still doing what I want to be doing?"

Your success rests on your adaptability—your ability and commitment to embrace change—and on your ability to actively manage your own career. Change, although frightening and intimidating at times, can also be very rewarding. Embracing change means pushing yourself to explore all the possibilities presented to you, including those that are easy to achieve and those that are a bit scary. What is your readiness for taking risks? The question is no longer "Can I change?", but rather "What type of change do I want?"

If you do not have some idea of what you want or where you want to go, you will more often be merely reacting to events as they occur, rather than controlling your direction. Having a vision helps us to guide our choices and direct our energy toward achieving our career goals. Many individuals have never considered that they can play a part in designing their own futures. Some may need to free themselves from a career path that others have expected them to follow before they can begin to formulate their own career visions. You must move away from thoughts of what others think you should be doing, which make you an observer of your career, and become an active participant in the picture—a goal setter, a "doer."

How to Create Your Career Vision

Wouldn't it be great to create your work the way you want it? Your career vision will be as individual as you are. Creating your career vision will require you to ask yourself some important questions, and to give yourself permission to let

> *"When you create your own future, there will always be risks. In life, neither growth nor gain comes without risk."*

> *"The indispensable first step to getting the things you want in this life is this: decide what you want."*
>
> Ben Stein

go of what you previously thought possible. Whereas scanning and assessing are concrete, tangible activities that set the context for a future plan, visioning is more abstract. Creating a vision is both the playful part of the career development process and the pivotal point upon which the planning and marketing phases depend.

Developing a career vision begins with taking time to do some active daydreaming about an ideal day in your future. When you start, your vision does not need to be too realistic; that comes later on, when you start to determine your options and set your career goals. Do not worry about whether your vision is too big, too vague, or too impossible; it should be grand and inspiring. If your dream is very important to you, it may also be a little scary. You should begin creating your career vision with the belief that your work can be all that you imagine. Ask yourself, "How can I become the best I can be?" "How can I combine my skills and talents with my dreams?" Having a clear vision of what you want for the future involves several steps. You must be able to form a mental picture of what it is you want and affirm your vision by articulating it verbally or in writing. Then you must be ready to commit to the vision you believe will occur and do what it takes to make it happen. With a clear vision that you are firmly committed to and the knowledge to bring it about, you will embark on a journey to discover your full potential.

ACTIVITY 4   Creating Your Career Vision

1. Career Wish List

This activity functions like a warm-up or brainstorming session to do before you really start to develop your vision. "Blue-sky thinking" is at work here; no answer is wrong. Have you always wanted to go back to school, to take on a management role, to work part-time, to chair a committee, or to start your own business? Can you think of someone else's situation that you would like to have? Connect with your imagination and creativity to make a list of what you really want, and what you are seeking. Then, after you have exhausted your list of dreams, start prioritizing them. If you had to choose between the first and second items on your list, which would you choose? Or, if you had to choose between items three and four, which would it be, and so on. Keep going until you have two or three significant career wants. You have not eliminated the other options; they have just become lower priorities.

2. My Ideal Vision for My Career

Visioning is a creative process that helps us to translate our dreams into words or pictures that can be used to communicate those dreams to others. The following are two ways to do this, one with words, and the other with pictures, that will help you focus when creating your vision story. As you answer the questions, your evolving career vision should be influenced, rather than determined, by the data you have gleaned from your scan and self-assessment.

Words. When you are ready, pretend it is a year or five years from now, and that you have achieved your career vision. Answer the following questions:

What does my ideal vision look like?

_____

_____

_____

_____

_____

_____

What am I doing?

_____

_____

_____

_____

_____

_____

Where am I doing it?

_____

_____

_____

_____

_____

_____

Who is there with me?

_____

_____

_____

_____

_____

_____

What talents and attributes am I using or expressing?

_____

_____

_____

_____

_____

How am I being acknowledged?

_____

_____

_____

_____

_____

_____

Now begin your vision story: "It is next year, or five years from now, and I am ..."

_____

_____

_____

_____

_____

_____

Pictures. What does your vision story look, feel, and sound like? Try to draw the vision or use pictures from magazines or other sources that represent your vision. Consider posting your pictures on a _vision board_ in a prominent place and revisit it every time you pass by. Add to and change the _vision board_ as new ideas emerge. Replay the vision in your head while you are waiting in line or doing tasks that do not require a lot of thought.

_____

_____

_____

_____

_____

> *"Our deepest fear is not that we are inadequate. Our deepest fear is that we are powerful beyond measure. It is our light, not our darkness that most frightens us. We ask ourselves, who am I to be brilliant, gorgeous, talented, fabulous? Actually, who are you not to be?"*
>
> Marianne Williamson

Self-Limiting Beliefs

At this juncture, you may be saying to yourself, "I want to (fill in your own response), but I cannot because (fill in your own response)." If this is happening, it is important to separate the real barriers (for example, "I am not qualified") from the perceived ones (for example, "I am too old"). Real barriers can generally be overcome, but perceived barriers, or self-limiting beliefs, will block our progress; these are the old, entrenched beliefs that oppose a new idea. What we believe about ourselves and what can be possible are powerful determinants of our behaviour. That is why it is so important to explore our assumptions and clarify the values that underpin them. Many of us believe that we cannot do what we really want to; we defeat our desires because we concentrate on why we "cannot" rather than why we "can." We may walk away from our dreams because we are afraid that we will fail or, worse yet, that we will succeed. If you are afraid of something (for example, taking on a leadership role), try to understand why it scares you, and then take action to overcome those feelings. Action cures fear; until you confront your fears, your dreams will never be as big as they can be. You must believe in your potential and yourself; the power of positive thinking cannot be underestimated. Think big!

ACTIVITY 5   Self-Limiting Beliefs

In the following table, list the self-limiting beliefs that are potentially getting in the way of your vision. Then, list possible strategies you can use to tackle each self-limiting belief.

SELF-LIMITING BELIEFS	
I cannot … (barriers)	I can … (enablers)
What self-limiting beliefs are blocking my career vision?	What is one strategy I can use to eliminate, or at least reduce, the impact of the barrier I have identified?
1.	1.
2.	2.
3.	3.

What Have You Accomplished?

Your career vision may be a confirmation that you are already doing what you love, or it may have shown you an entirely new way to think about expressing yourself in your work. You are more likely to attain a satisfying career when you follow your personal passions, pursue your interests, and utilize your strengths. Go back to your scanning exercise and your self-assessment. Does your career vision fit with what the new world of work requires, and with the skills, talents, and abilities you have to offer? If so, then you now have a vision of what you want to build and you can move forward as quickly or as slowly as you desire. If not, you have not wasted your time. Review your scan, your self-assessment, and your career vision. If your vision still appears realistic, it may be that the timing is just not right. Do not let go of your vision; be patient yet persistent, and take smaller steps. Make adjustments so that you are positioned to take advantage of better circumstances when the climate changes and opportunities arise. Surround yourself with people who will support and encourage you, even while your career vision might appear impossible.

Now list three things that you have learned from Phase Three:

1. _____

2. _____

3. _____

Did anything surprise you? How? Why?

_____

_____

_____

_____

_____

Identify one thing you currently do that will be influenced by what you have learned from creating your career vision.

_____

_____

_____

_____

_____

_____

What is one thing that you would like to follow up on?

_____

_____

_____

_____

_____

_____

To keep you on track and your eye on the horizon, restate your career vision here.

I AM ... _____

_____

_____

_____

_____

_____

What Is Your Next Step?

Today, career success depends not only on having a dream, but also on knowing how to turn that dream into a reality. Phase Four, *Developing Your Strategic Career Plan,* will help you answer the question "How will I get there from here?" This section will provide you with strategies to close the gap between vision and reality. You will learn to set clear goals that will convert your dreams into actions, and to see these actions as steps toward designing your strategic career plan. Go for it!

planning

PHASE FOUR

Developing Your
Strategic Career Plan

*Chance favours the
prepared mind.*

Louis Pasteur

What Is a Strategic Career Plan?

A strategic career plan is a blueprint for action; it specifies the activities, timelines, and resources you need to help you achieve your career vision and goals. Although chance occurrences may play a role in shaping your career, planning and preparation will put you in a position to take full advantage of chance occurrences, to recognize opportunity, and to assess risk. This is the part of the development process where you start to document the strategies you will use to take charge of your future. Of course, this is also where the iterative nature of the career planning process is reinforced. You should be constantly scanning your environment, assessing yourself, and re-evaluating your goals and plans for reaching those goals.

A career is a lifelong investment and, as with any investment, planning pays off! In this section, you will learn how to create your own career plan and how to implement it. Getting started signals your commitment to acting on a specific goal. Also, beginning to plan indicates that you are ready to address each component required to make your plan successful, and that you are serious about embarking on the journey toward your overall vision.

Why Is Planning Important?

A plan provides you with an answer to the question "How do I achieve my goals?" A plan is like a map outlining a series of specific goal-directed activities that will, over time, guide you to your destination. By having a well-developed action plan, you will be able to recognize and take advantage of career opportunities when they occur. Without a plan, career goals may appear unattainable or become that way. Although it may take time to achieve your vision, having a plan will help to ensure that you are continuously moving in the right direction.

> *"Vision without action is only a dream; action without vision only passes the time; but vision with action can change the world."*
> Joel Barker

By creating a plan, you begin to move forward and to make decisions. Each decision builds on the previous ones and leads to actions, and each of these actions then affect the choices you will have in the future. As you proceed through your strategic career plan, the incremental steps you take to achieve your goals will become recognizable, and each one you complete will provide you with an incentive to persevere.

How to Develop a Strategic Career Plan

A strategic career plan is predicated on your career vision and includes goals, action steps, timelines, resources needed, and indicators of success. It is important to document your plan in writing—the exercise of "writing it down" forces you to include each critical component and makes it easier for you to review, refine, evaluate, and re-evaluate your goals and progress regularly. Remember that the only way your plan will remain useful to you is if you continually assess whether it reflects what you want to achieve in light of changes to your environment, self, and career stage. Writing down your plan also helps you make a commitment to yourself—that you will work on making your plan a reality. To create your plan, you will need to dedicate some time, energy, and creativity. Do not worry if the plan you write is not perfect—it is a work in progress.

Setting Your Career Goals

The first step in career planning is to make a decision, even if it is a tentative one, about one or more of your career goals. A goal is the purpose or objective toward which an endeavour is directed; it is a dream taken seriously. Goals are steps toward your vision. In previous parts of this handbook, you answered questions related to where you would like to go and your ideal vision for your work. What was it that you wanted to change or accomplish? Goals are the foundation for sound planning and for taking smart, calculated risks. Your success in whatever you choose to do depends on your ability to set goals because this will keep you looking toward the future and focused on doing it all, and doing it right. If you do not set goals, your career vision will forever remain a dream. Choosing and setting goals means that you are serious about taking charge of your career.

When setting goals, it is important to remember that a goal is a concrete action or event; it is a matter of facts, not feelings. For example, if one of your long-term goals is to join the board of directors of your national professional organization, a short-term goal toward this end is to volunteer on a committee at the local level. You can concentrate on one goal at a time or pursue several at once. Pursuing multiple goals encourages flexibility and helps you to feel more in control and less at the mercy of external forces, for example, organizational change, because it gives you a "backup plan" in the event that your desired direction becomes blocked. Career goals should be realistic ("I can do it"), desirable ("I want to do it"), and motivating ("I will work to make it happen"). Remember that you will re-evaluate and alter your career goals as you move toward your career vision, and you may even change your vision as you encounter new experiences in your professional life. Even if your vision does change, you can still build on the activities and resources you have used to meet the goals that were a part of that vision. Setting clear goals involves converting your dream from a vague idea into an action-oriented goal statement and then using that to design your strategic career plan. For example, using the above scenario, you might say to yourself, "I will be a member of a national professional board of directors before I reach age 45, and I will become involved in a local professional policy development committee within the year."

My career goal is:

_____

_____

_____

_____

_____

Now look at your goal. Is it:

- Achievable and realistic?   YES ☐ NO ☐

If not, then you may be setting yourself up for disappointment.

- Specific enough?   YES ☐ NO ☐

If not, then it will be difficult to identify an action plan to achieve your goal. Vague goals do not set plans into action.

- Supported by those who will be directly
  affected by your decision, including
  partners, family, colleagues, and friends?   YES ☐ NO ☐

If not, then you may miss an opportunity to surround yourself with a network of allies who can help you achieve your goals.

Formulating Your Action Steps

A career plan is more effective when it is broken down into specific, manageable "action steps" that make the plan feel less overwhelming. These steps are like building blocks for achieving well-defined goals. Action steps also help you to track the progress of your plan and are tangible evidence that you are moving in the right direction. These action steps are the "how-to" strategies for achieving your career goals. In keeping with the above example, some action steps might sound like this: "In order to become involved in a local professional policy development committee, I will contact my professional organization to inquire about any openings, and to find out how to apply."

Identifying Your Resources

The most effective career plans are not developed in isolation. Once you have decided on your career plan, it is important to examine the available resources and opportunities within your environment that

Resource Inventory

- *Whom should I talk to?*
- *What should I read?*
- *Where should I spend some time?*
- *What do I need to invest?*

may help you. You can access information from the Internet, newspapers, professional publications and organizations, career centres, workshops, and your network of peers and mentors. Taking a thoughtful inventory of the resources available to you should be the first action step you take toward reaching each of your goals.

Establishing Your Timelines

It is important to set a realistic timeline for each of your action steps. If your goal is personally motivating and your plan is realistic and concrete, assigning timelines ensures that you allocate your resources in an efficient and, ultimately, a rewarding way. Timelines should be suited to your particular needs and fit your personal priorities. Although timelines can be modified, including them at the outset is critical to developing an effective career plan.

Identifying Your Indicators of Success

How will you know that your plan is working? The indicators of success that you identify will help you to evaluate your plan at different stages of your career. If you have identified your goals and documented your plan, including specific action steps, required resources, and timelines, you have made a good start toward measuring your success. Think about what you hope to accomplish with your plan. Completing a specific action step that clearly moves you toward your goal may make you feel that your plan is proving to be effective. Assessing that you are professionally stimulated and happy doing what you are doing while you work through the plan may also show that you have developed it successfully. Another sign of having set a good plan is that you feel you have taken charge of your own career. As you design your career plan, think about what success will look like for you, keeping in mind that you may define success differently at various stages of your career.

 **Developing Your Strategic Career Plan**

Now you are ready to develop your own strategic career plan. Start by thinking about the career vision you set in Phase Three. Then, work your way through the exercise in the following table. Repeat for each career goal.

DEVELOPING A STRATEGIC CAREER PLAN

MY CAREER VISION:

Career Goal #	Timeline Accomplish by:

Indicator of Success
I know I will have succeeded in this goal when:

Action Steps In order to achieve this goal I will:	Resources

Once you have clarified your goals, a plan and appropriate follow-up can be developed. Remember:

- *When you are formulating your plan, be specific about who, what, when, and where.*

- *Be accountable; take responsibility for your plan.*

- *Communicate your vision, how you want to take action, and your need for help.*

- *Stop often to reflect, and to identify anticipated successes and the steps that will follow.*

- *Keep your vision "front and centre."*

What Have You Accomplished?

Setting a strategic career plan is a comprehensive way to work toward reaching your career vision. With a well-developed career plan, you will be able to define your goals and the action steps needed to achieve them. Your career plan will enable you to be proactive—it will assist you in taking risks and facing your internal and exterior barriers. Your plan will also allow you to recognize and take advantage of career opportunities when they occur.

Your career plan belongs to you—you have created it based on your dreams. As your dreams change, so will your plan; throughout the span of your career, you will continually modify your plan as new opportunities arise, and as growth is achieved. With a carefully developed career plan you will be well on your way to taking control of your future.

Now list three things that you have learned from Phase Four:

1. _____

2. _____

3. _____

Did anything surprise you? How? Why?

_____

_____

_____

_____

_____

Identify one thing you currently do that will be influenced by what you have learned from developing your strategic career plan.

_____

_____

_____

_____

_____

What is one thing you would like to follow up on?

_____

_____

_____

_____

_____

What Is Your Next Step?

You have a vision; you know your current strengths, values, interests, and accomplishments; you know how they fit with the world of health care; you have a goal; and you have a plan. Congratulations! This has been hard work, so it is important to recognize and reward yourself for your successes. Also, keep re-evaluating—and possibly altering—your career plan to achieve the career vision you have developed, and start telling others about your ideas. Now you are ready for Phase Five, *Marketing Yourself*, which will help you strategize further to achieve your goals.

marketing

PHASE FIVE

Marketing Yourself

What Is Marketing?

Just as you help your clients to articulate their needs, so must you learn to speak for yourself when aiming to successfully implement your career plans. Marketing, which can take numerous forms and be used for many purposes, helps you to present yourself so that others recognize who you are and what you have to offer. Regardless of whether your career goal involves choosing a role as an employee, deciding to embark on private practice, becoming an entrepreneur, or volunteering on a committee in your workplace or community, you will need to acquire marketing skills.

Self-marketing involves the ability to package your professional and personal attributes, including your expertise, so that you can effectively communicate why you are the best person to deliver a particular service. Additionally, self-marketing includes scanning your environment and "knowing your business." However, being able to articulate who you are, what you want, and what you can do is only half of the equation when applying marketing principles in the health care sector; the other half is being able to persuade others that what you can offer meets the demands and challenges of the changing environment.

Why Is Marketing Important?

Searching for opportunities (paid or volunteer) in the twenty-first century is not simply about sending out résumés and answering ads. You must also have a specific set of strategies that position you to get what you want. In completing your self-assessment, you will have identified your values and beliefs, your past experiences and accomplishments, and your strengths and areas for improvement. You can now use these facts to determine how you want to present or market yourself to others in order to meet your career goals. Marketing strategies include making yourself visible, establishing a network, finding a mentor, and enhancing your written and verbal communication skills. When marketing yourself, you are in control of how you present yourself, and to whom; you choose what it is you want other people to know about you. Developing a self-marketing strategy can assist you to move from the planning phase to the results phase in achieving your career goals. The purpose of this section is to provide you with an overview of some key marketing strategies that you can use to realize your career vision.

> *"Even if you are on the right track, you will get run over if you just sit there."*
> Will Rogers

The Product Is You!

Throughout your daily interactions with clients, peers, and other professionals, whether in person, on the phone, or via e-mail, you have many opportunities as a health professional to present yourself to others and to influence them. As you do this, you send a particular message about who you are, based on an image you have created. In fact, you are your own best marketer. How you look, conduct yourself, and speak governs your first impression on others, and so these things are critical to self-marketing. Presenting yourself is not about trying to be someone else, but about presenting the person you are in the best possible light. Before you begin to use any of the marketing tools and strategies that are available, consider the "product" that is you. It is often uncomfortable to think of marketing ourselves because we think it means manipulating or deceiving others. However, self-marketing is actually exactly the opposite: it is having confidence in who we are and in what we want to do, and then projecting that to others. Understanding yourself is the first step to marketing yourself.

Networking

Networking is about building relationships with others to meet career goals; it is a mutual process that may involve exchanging information or resources with others, which can happen in person or in writing. This process is also about asking others to help you achieve what you want by gathering information on your behalf, providing referrals, or passing on information about new opportunities. Networking is key to staying informed about what is happening in the world, and to understanding how emerging trends and issues will affect your work. This knowledge will help you position yourself strategically and maintain your professional visibility.

You can start the process of developing a network by thinking of people who share your values and interests, and who may be helpful to you and vice versa—colleagues, managers, previous teachers or mentors, clinical colleagues, human resources staff, and friends may all be included. Think especially of others who are doing the type of work that you would like to do. Once you have made a list of people to include in your network, contact them; be specific about what you are looking for and what you would like them to do for you. Also, remember to express who you are and what you can do for them. Who you know is not as important as who knows you—other people need to know who you are in order to help you. After speaking or meeting with an individual, always leave with the names of three other people to contact.

Building your network is an ongoing process, and the people in your network will change over time. Continue to develop your network by participating in committees and projects, attending workshops or conferences, and doing volunteer work. Formal education and involvement in professional organizations can also help to expand your professional network. Take advantage of opportunities to meet, speak with, and learn about others. You never know where new relationships may lead.

> *How can anyone help you unless you let them know what you want? When you share your career vision, your network enlarges and the probability of success increases.*

Finding a Mentor

Acquiring a mentor from inside or outside of the health care sector can provide you with the additional support and guidance that you need to transform your career dreams into reality. Mentors are often individuals who are more experienced and have more access to information than their less-experienced colleagues; also, they typically have a large network and good connections. Mentors are interested in sharing their knowledge and fostering leadership skills in professionals who are newer to their careers. They can support you in scanning your environment, conducting your self-assessment, and developing a specific career plan. Also, they may be able to help you learn ways to become more politically savvy and to meet the right people, opening doors that will lead you to success by enhancing your professional visibility.

You may feel uncomfortable about approaching a potential mentor. However, keep in mind that mentors also benefit from a relationship with their protegés; the process gives them an opportunity to contribute to their profession (and, on a grander scale, to society) by developing others and helping those people to expand their networks. The clearer you are about why you want a mentor and what purpose the relationship will serve for you, the easier it will be to find someone who is willing and a very good fit. See Appendix E for more information about coaching and mentoring.

Marketing Yourself in Writing

There are many ways to market yourself with written material. Résumés and cover letters, curricula vitae (CVs), business cards, Web sites, blogs, and writing for publication are the most popular.

Résumés

A well-constructed résumé is an important part of self-marketing. It represents your knowledge, skills, and achievements in such a convincing way that readers can get an immediate sense of who you are and what you can do for them. A résumé creates a first impression in writing, and its main purpose is to bring you an opportunity to present yourself in person—an interview. Résumés may be required to apply for a range of opportunities, such as positions within an organization, seats on a committee inside or outside of your organization, and the chance to work with a group of independent health professionals.

Creating a résumé requires time, patience, and practice. There is no such thing as a generic or "one-size-fits-all" résumé. To be most effective, your résumé must be customized for each opportunity you pursue, and it should include components of your self-assessment—that is, your knowledge, skills, and specific and measurable achievements. Before customizing a résumé, you need to know something about the position for which you are applying. What qualifications are being sought, and how do your knowledge, skills, and accomplishments relate to the position? It is also helpful to know something about the organization at this point; for example, what are the organization's values related to care? Does your résumé reflect similar values? In Appendix B you will find a summary of résumé types, a sample résumé outline, and tips for electronic résumés.

The Cover Letter

A résumé must always be accompanied by a one-page cover letter, either in print or as an attachment if the rest of your application is electronic. The purpose of a cover letter is to encourage its recipients to read your résumé in more detail, and thus determine how your experience and abilities can benefit their organization. In today's competitive and rapidly changing world of work, you must express clear goals and use creative strategies when designing a cover letter. Also, the letter should be written after your résumé, but should not be a repetition of the résumé itself. Remember, the goal of your cover letter is to convince readers that they will benefit from looking at your application more closely.

What Is the Difference Between a Résumé and a Curriculum Vitae?

The terms *résumé* and *curriculum vitae* (CV) are often used interchangeably, but they are actually two different types of documents. Whereas a résumé is a summary document of usually two to three pages that highlights your education, professional background, and accomplishments, a CV is a detailed and all-encompassing document that describes your professional and academic interests while reflecting your entire career to date. A CV is usually used to apply for grants, scholarships, awards, and academic appointments;

a résumé, on the other hand, is most often used to apply for a specific position. If you are unsure as to which document is required for an application, you can always call the organization to clarify. An outline for a CV can be found in Appendix C.

Business Cards

Another self-marketing strategy to consider is a personal business card. You may already have business cards related to your current position, but these will not be appropriate if you are in the process of looking for alternative opportunities. Having a personal business card to offer when you are networking with others is more impressive than fumbling with pen and paper. Your business card represents who you are, so you want it to be attractive and look professional. Your card should include your name, credentials, street and e-mail addresses, and telephone and fax numbers. You can create your business cards on your home computer or your hand-held device, or you can purchase them through a print shop, which is typically quick and inexpensive.

Web Sites, Blogs, and Writing for Publication

In our technological age, many individuals use the Internet as a marketing vehicle as well as a vehicle for communication. A personal Web site allows you to describe yourself and your skills, knowledge, and accomplishments in your own words, and in a more informal way than, for example, a résumé. A Web site can also include photos of you, examples of your publications, and testimonials from others. If you choose to have a Web site, you must keep it updated; if you are not able or willing to put the time into maintaining a site, you are best advised not to have one.

A blog is a type of Web site used by people who want to share their experiences and ideas. It is like your own personal editorial page—a place where you can talk about the issues of interest to you. As with a Web site, be sure you will be able to keep it current. Also, remember that you never know who will be looking at your

Web site or your blog, so if you are not willing to be accountable for everything you say or show, it is best to avoid these particular marketing strategies.

Writing about your work offers further opportunities to market your knowledge and skills. There are a variety of places where you may publish your writing, both in print and online. Your first publication does not need to be in a scholarly, peer-reviewed journal; it could be in your workplace or professional association's newsletter, or in the "letters to the editor" section of your local or national newspaper.

What can you write about? Health professionals can focus on various aspects of their work, such as new methods of delivering care, outcomes as a result of care, career satisfaction, how to demonstrate leadership, and how to influence others. Write about what you know, or how you make a difference. Writing demonstrates your knowledge regarding a specific issue; for this reason, be sure to include your contact information anywhere you publish so that others can reach you for more information. Any chance to present your knowledge and abilities in writing creates further opportunities for self-marketing.

> *"Let me tell you the secret that has led me to my goal: my strength lies solely in my tenacity."*
>
> Louis Pasteur

Marketing Yourself in Person

This section describes some of the strategies you can use to market yourself in person, including interviewing, making presentations, and acting as a mentor. With all of these strategies, it is important to keep in mind that how you feel about and present yourself are critical when self-marketing.

The Interview

Today, the interview is a crucial step in landing either a new job or a position on a board or committee—this is where the final decision is made. The interview process has become more complex than it once was, and everyone, including health professionals, must be prepared to sell themselves and their skills in a variety of ways.

There are various types of interviews—single, panel, serial, and telephone—as well as types of interview questions. Traditional questions involve queries and answers, behavioural questions probe specific past behaviours, and situational questions ask interviewees to respond to specific situations that they may be faced with in the role. Getting an interview is a sign that someone thinks you have the qualifications for the position. Still, it is up to you to present and "sell" yourself as the best candidate. The interview is your opportunity to convince others that there is a strong fit between your skills and knowledge and those required by the position. You must clearly articulate what skills you have to offer and how you have demonstrated those skills through past experience.

Preparation is essential for a successful interview. Investing time and effort can ultimately result in an offer. For a sample of potential questions you may be asked, or that you should consider asking, please see Appendix D. Each of your interview situations presents a valuable learning experience. Review your interview when it is over and make notes for future interview preparation. Some questions to consider include the following: "How did the interview go?" "Did I feel confident or unprepared?" "What went well?" "What would I change for the next time?", and "What can I take from this experience to my next interview?" Alternatively, you might review the interview with a colleague, career coach, or mentor who can give you support and constructive feedback. If you were unsuccessful in being offered a position, you might also seek feedback from the interviewer, if possible.

Making Presentations

Health professionals can use presentations as another strategy to market themselves. You can present the same issues that work well when writing for publication, presenting, for example, how you have made a difference to care delivery, how you have implemented a new clinical practice, or what you have found when researching. There are many opportunities to participate in both formal and informal presentations that occur in a variety of settings, and for a variety of occasions.

In your workplace, informal opportunities to present may include conducting an education session for peers or for students within your program. Opportunities may also include the impromptu teaching you do with clients, families, and students on a daily basis. Formal presentations in your workplace could involve presenting rounds or delivering staff or client education programs.

Outside of your workplace, and even your profession, there are many opportunities for marketing your skills and knowledge to colleagues and leaders through presentations. Forums may include professional conferences and workshops, where you may deliver a paper or poster presentation, or advisory committees, where you have the opportunity to work on professional or government policy. Alternatively, you may consider teaching in an educational program, even as a guest lecturer, so that you may share your knowledge and expertise. The more often you are visible, the more people will get to know you and what you have to offer. Who knows? Your ventures outside of your primary workplace may lead to other career and networking opportunities.

Acting as a Mentor

While seeking a mentor may help you to achieve your career goals, acting as a mentor can do the same. If one of your goals is to share your knowledge and expertise with other professionals, then why not volunteer to be a mentor? A true mentor–protegé relationship should be mutually beneficial; while sharing your expertise, you may also learn from your protegé. Being a mentor may not seem like a self-marketing opportunity, but you will, in fact, be building your network when you share your knowledge, skills, and accomplishments with a less-experienced colleague.

ACTIVITY 7   Marketing Yourself

Now that you have read about the range of marketing strategies, think about your marketing readiness. Check off the items that you feel confident about; for the others, ask yourself, "What do I need to do?" and "When will I do it?"

MARKETING READINESS

I know that I am my own best marketer. ☐

I know how to network. ☐

I either have a mentor or I am one myself. ☐

I have a current résumé. ☐

I have a personal business card. ☐

I have recently made a presentation. ☐

I have been published or I am working toward this goal. ☐

I have excellent interviewing skills. ☐

WHAT I NEED TO DO

WHEN I WILL DO IT

What Have You Accomplished?

Self-marketing is about using various resources to present yourself in the most positive way. This section has provided you with a variety of strategies to help you market yourself, both in writing and in person. To be effective, the tools presented here must incorporate what you have learned in your self-assessment and must truly represent who you are and what you have to offer. Creating effective tools (for example, résumés, cover letters, and business cards) and enhancing your interview skills helps you to develop a positive professional image that can give you an edge in your search for rewarding career opportunities. Understanding how to create a self-marketing plan is the key to career success, no matter what the stage of your career. Remember, you are your own best resource and your own best cheerleader. You have control over how you present and market yourself to others, both now and in the future.

Now list three things that you have learned from Phase Five:

1. _____

2. _____

3. _____

Did anything surprise you? How? Why?

_____

_____

_____

_____

_____

_____

Identify one thing you currently do that will be influenced by what you have learned from the marketing strategies.

_____

_____

_____

_____

_____

_____

What is one thing that you would like to follow up on?

_____

_____

_____

_____

_____

What Is Your Next Step?

To ensure that you are getting the most out of the career planning process, you should consider regularly evaluating how your career planning activities are working for you. Doing this will help you to determine which phases of the model need more of your attention, whether your plan needs updating, and whether you should seek more consultation and support. Next is the Career Readiness Checklist—these are the same questions you asked yourself at the start of this career planning journey. Complete this now, and then again after each career change or on an annual basis.

CAREER READINESS ✓ Checklist

Scanning

☐ I am aware of the current realities and future trends within health care and my profession at the local, national, and global levels.

☐ I am aware of the local, national, and global realities and future trends from outside health care and my profession that can impact the way I work and how the health care system works.

Assessing

☐ I can articulate my values as they relate to my career.

☐ I can describe my strengths and how I use them in my work.

☐ I can describe my limitations.

☐ I know how others would describe me.

☐ I can describe three significant accomplishments I have made in the past three to five years.

☐ My current position is a good match with my values, beliefs, knowledge, skills, and interests.

☐ I make time to do the things that are important to me in my personal life.

Visioning

☐ I can describe my ideal vision or visions for my work.

Planning

☐ I can identify career goals that are related to my vision.

☐ I have a written career development plan in place.

☐ I know what steps to take over the next six to twelve months to further my career.

Marketing

❑ I have established a relevant network.

❑ I have, or am considering acquiring, a mentor or a coach.

❑ I continue to develop my communication skills through written and oral presentations.

❑ I have an up-to-date résumé.

What changes have occurred since the most recent time you filled out the checklist? Are you feeling more confident? More in control of your career? More career-resilient? If so, this is exactly what we had hoped for. Now you will need to keep up your momentum; the next section offers some suggestions on how you might do this.

Part Five

Sustaining Your Career Plan

> *It is easy enough to go off on a quest, but to return—well, that is another story. What has been gained can still be lost at this point.* Joseph Campbell

The process of integrating your plan into reality can be either smooth or rocky. For instance, the career vision you have now articulated for yourself may take you in a completely new direction from where you began. Also, you will need to defend the insights you have gained against all of those "voices"—both yours and others'—that may dampen your enthusiasm for what could be.

Just having taken the risk of embarking on this journey may encourage you to stick to your plan. Also, reflecting on the questions you answered during the planning process will give you some insight into the question "What now?", and this will help you. Still, you will need resources, support, and feedback when you re-enter your day-to-day world, but from where, and from whom? Several strategies exist for finding support while you are re-evaluating your career. For example, you might go online or visit your local library or bookstore to scan the myriad of career planning and development resources. (We have included a listing of some of our favourite resources in Appendix F.) Another strategy that can help you to sustain your vision and plans is to establish a *support group,* either in "real time" or online. This "career support team" would be there on the sidelines, encouraging you as you take steps toward your vision. A support group provides the opportunity to speak and be heard—to discuss with others your struggles, fears, dreams, and discoveries by naming and describing these experiences. What becomes evident when working with a support group is that you are not alone, and that you can make your needs known to others. The more you express what you want and need from others, the easier it is for those people to help you. For all of us, the power of shared intention is significant.

Your support group may include people in your network along with others who are interested in supporting you as you work to achieve your career goals. Select people for your group who are positive and who will contribute to your confidence. Of course, also include individuals whom you want to help as well. Use your support group for honest feedback and emotional support when you need extra encouragement, such as when you are feeling uncertain about taking a risk.

You may also benefit from a more formalized follow-up through individual *career coaching*. If you are contemplating a significant career or personal change, a continuous coaching relationship can help you to keep on track. The idea "I can do it on my own" is not unfamiliar to health professionals who are used to providing guidance and help to others, and so needing help ourselves is sometimes difficult to acknowledge. Coaching is not advice-giving, teaching, or directing. Rather, the coaching process is a collaboration in which the coach acts like a midwife, supporting, encouraging, and helping you through an experience while acknowledging you as the expert—the person "making it happen." Because coaching is really a conversation built on mutual trust, choose a coach whose expertise and approach you are comfortable with, and that you value. Health care, professional, and community organizations may include coaching services as part of their offerings. Of course, many independent coaches also practise on a fee-for-service basis. Just as in any other relationship, the fit between you and your coach is critical. For this reason, when you are looking for someone to work with, use your network, get some referrals, and then search out a few potential coaches. Learn as much as you can about how each one works, what training, experience, and expertise they have (in- and outside of health care), and their fees, if required. See Appendix E for more information.

> *"And the end of all our exploring will be to arrive where we started and know the place for the first time."*
> Thomas Stearns Eliot

You should now have a thorough understanding of the Donner–Wheeler Career Planning and Development Model and how to use it. Attending to your professional development is a time-intensive process that requires reflection as well as planning. The career planning process presented in this handbook gives you a way of relating your ideas and visions to the practical realities of your life in order to achieve useful and realizable outcomes. The plan allows you to get the most out of yourself and your career while also giving the best possible care to your clients. The career planning process is really about developing life skills that you can apply not only in your workplace, but also in your personal life. While this handbook is presented as a personal guide, it can also be shared with family and friends. A career needs attention and nurturing; this handbook is intended to provide you with the skills you need in order to care for yourself and your career. Your future is in your hands.

Appendix A

Assessment Tools

If the services of a professional are required to complement your self-assessment, a career coach can help you to assess your strengths and dominant traits objectively and relative to your work environment, using a variety of well-researched and developed techniques. It is helpful to familiarize yourself with the spectrum of assessment tools available, what they assess, and which ones will align best with your career development plans. Most assessments are available online, are scored automatically, and produce user-friendly reports. While some must be administered by a psychologist, there are many assessments available that you can do yourself, at home.

An assessment has the most impact when it is followed up by a discussion with a career coach or expert, about the tool you have used and any reports related to its use. The expert can relate the feedback from your assessment back to your specific development needs. Standardized tests can also be used in combination with your self-assessment. These tests can identify your strengths, which you will want to optimize, and also alert you to potential areas of weakness, or "blind spots," so that you can minimize their impact on your work. Assessing yourself (or being assessed) may change your perceptions of who you are and what you want, and can open doors to new roles or career opportunities that you may not have otherwise known or thought about. Look for assessment tools that are reliable and valid, and that are clear about what they are assessing.

The following is a list of some aspects of a person that can be assessed and, for each, an example of a well-known test that you may want to consider:

1. Cognitive intelligence or IQ:
    *   Wonderlic Personnel Test (WPT)
        www.wonderlic.com

2. Emotional intelligence:
    *   EQ-I (Emotion Quotient Inventory)
        www.mhs.com/mhs

3. Personality and interests:
    *   Myers-Briggs Type Indicator (MBTI)
        www.myersbriggs.org
    *   Campbell Interest and Skill Survey (CISS)
        www.pearsonassessments.com/tests/ciss.htm
    *   Strong Interest Inventory
        www.psychometrics.com

4. Working styles:
    *   Working Style Analysis (WSA)
        www.creativelearningcentre.com/products/working-style-analysis

5. Career direction and related self-knowledge:
    *   Thomas Personal Profile Analysis (PPA) Test
        www.thomasus.com
    *   Career Occupational Preference System (COPS)
        www.edits.net/career.html
    *   Career Orientation Placement and Evaluation Survey (COPES)
        www.edits.net/copes.html
    *   True Colors
        www.truecolors.org

Assessment services may be available to you at no cost from many sources: through an employee assistance program or career development centre associated with your workplace, through a relocation or outplacement firm, through your local university or college, through the YMCA, YWCA, or other community organization, or over the Internet. Do your research on any assessment tools and career development specialists you are considering. For career coaches or specialists, also secure references from satisfied clients. Then, make your choice based on sound information and a comfortable fit with the professional, ensuring that both are well aligned with your personal style, your career needs, and your aspirations.

Résumé Tips

Types of Résumés

In general, there are two basic résumé styles: chronological and functional. Some people prefer to combine the two styles into what is often referred to as a hybrid style.

Chronological Style

This format is the most common and represents the more traditional type of résumé. In a chronological résumé, work history and education are described with dates in reverse-chronological order, with the most recent experiences appearing first. This style is most often used to demonstrate career progression by showing positions of increased responsibility or academic preparation.

Functional Style

A functional résumé highlights an individual's skills and accomplishments. This style allows an applicant the opportunity to accentuate transferable skills, and puts less emphasis on previous jobs or academic preparation, allowing the applicant to highlight qualifications and skills specific to what the employer wants. A functional résumé may be especially useful if you are aiming to change your role, perhaps to something non-traditional, or are seeking employment outside of the health care sector.

Hybrid Style

A hybrid résumé combines the strengths of both chronological and functional résumés. This type of résumé emphasizes career continuity, as in the chronological style, and also highlights expertise and accomplishments, as in the functional style.

Creating Your Résumé

This section explains what information to include under each of the potential headings in a chronological résumé. Remember that these are guidelines; you can tailor the sections of your résumé to your liking, or to the needs of a particular position.

Contact Information

Here, write your name, designations, street and e-mail addresses, telephone number, and fax number (if you have one).

Career Objective or a Career Summary

This is a concise statement of what you are looking for. For example, you might write that you are, "Seeking a leadership position with a community organization that is making a focused, strategic difference in chronic illness management." A career summary creates a strong positive impression by summarizing strengths, accomplishments, expertise, and career interests.

Education

Include any degrees, diplomas, and certificates granted here, including the names and locations of the granting institutions and the dates.

Honours and Awards

Honours or awards from your workplace, academic institution, or professional association can be included here.

Work Experience

Describe your ongoing contributions and accomplishments here by providing information that reflects your career progression.

Professional Development

In this section, only include professional development activities relevant to the position for which you are applying; label this section, "Selected Professional Development Activities."

Professional Memberships and Affiliations

Include any offices or leadership positions you have held here.

Publications and Presentations

If you have written for numerous publications, provide the ones that are most recent and relevant. (Anything from the past seven years is considered appropriate.) Keep in mind that as a member of a research team, you are entitled to be cited as a contributor on anything published regarding the collaboration as long as you played a role in the work.

Community/Volunteer Experience

Include experiences here that are relevant to the type of work you are seeking. It is useful to include volunteer experience that has provided you with skills that you may not have developed in your paid work.

References

It is not desirable to include the names of references on your résumé, although they are commonly included. Just like everything else in your résumé, you want your references to be relevant to the position and the organization in question. If an employer requires references before an interview, you can include them in writing.

Using Technology: Electronic Résumés

Technology has had a huge impact on the job-search process, and health care has not been excluded. An electronic résumé is an important self-marketing tool; in fact, many hiring managers and recruiters prefer to receive résumés by e-mail. What exactly is an electronic résumé? E-résumés come in various formats; you might send an MS Word attachment, a document in plain text, or a PDF file. Alternatively, you might post your résumé on a job board or send a combined Web résumé and portfolio on a CD-ROM or through a Weblink.

Use key words when constructing your résumé. Key words are words associated with a specific industry, profession, or job function, and clearly and succinctly communicate a specific message. Currently, in health care, key words such as "teamwork," "interpersonal skills," "patient safety," and "patient care" are commonly used. To find key words, review job postings, corporate Web sites, classified ads, and job descriptions.

To e-mail a résumé successfully, you must put the file into the proper electronic format. Be sure to check which format the employer requires. While technology may save time for individuals when applying for positions, it also poses risks, such as accidentally attaching viruses or corrupt files. Make sure that your anti-virus protection is up to date, and always follow up electronic files with a hard copy.

Outline for a Curriculum Vitae (CV)

Contact Information

Include your name, designations, street and e-mail addresses, telephone number, and fax number (if you have one).

Education

Record degrees, certificates, and diplomas granted here, including the names and locations of the granting institutions and the dates.

Academic Honours and Awards

Include the name of each award, the date it was granted, and the name of the granting agency.

Professional and Community Honours and Awards

This category may be combined with the one above or appear independently, listing the same details as for academic honours and awards.

Current Position

List your position title and your employer or employing agency here. If yours is an academic position, follow this section with sections on undergraduate courses you have taught, graduate courses you have taught, and Masters or PhD students you have supervised.

Previous Positions

List the position titles, employing agencies, and a brief description of each role here.

Funded Research

In this section, include the grant name, granting agency, and amount of each grant you have received.

Publications

Here, use a consistent and recognizable format to list your publications, for example, the APA style. Use the following subsections: "Peer-Reviewed," "Chapters in Books," "Book Reviews," and "Other Publications."

Academic Presentations

Include peer-reviewed abstracts or papers in this section.

Professional and Community Presentations

Include speeches and non-refereed papers here.

Peer-Reviewed Activities

Record grant reviews and journal reviews in this section.

University/Academic Boards and Committees

This section can be divided into university-wide and faculty or department categories; list each one.

Professional Consultations

Here, list work you have done for organizations, professional associations, and the like.

Professional Boards and Committees

This section could include membership on professional organization and community agency boards and committees. Be sure to indicate whether you are a chair or executive on any of the boards or committees you mention.

Community Service

Any volunteer activities not related to your profession or health care could be added here.

Special Appointments

Any government or other appointments that you want to highlight separately can be listed here.

Interview Tips

Preparing for the Interview

1. Find out what type of interview to expect. How many people will be interviewing you? Who is the contact person?

2. Confirm the date, time, and location of the interview, particularly if an organization has more than one site. On the day of the interview, be sure you know how to get to the interview site and allow extra time to get there.

3. Do some research about the organization you aim to join: What are its values, mission, and philosophy? What is its strategic plan? Has there been a recent change in the organization's senior leadership, or its board of directors? Is the organization downsizing, merging, or expanding its programs? Have there been any recent staff layoffs? Much of this information can be found on an employer's Web site.

4. Review the ad or job description of the position for which you are being interviewed. Make sure you are able to articulate how your skills, expertise, and accomplishments meet the position requirements.

5. Anticipate potential questions that you may be asked during the interview and prepare answers to those questions. Prepare some questions to ask the interviewers. Please see "Questions ... A Two-Way Street" (below) for examples.

6. Practise interviewing with a friend, colleague, mentor, instructor, or career coach. Ask for feedback on how you answered their questions. This can be a very helpful strategy if done in a serious but non-threatening manner.

7. Bring extra copies of your résumé to the interview.

8. Contact your references ahead of the interview. Brief them after the interview.

9. Be polite and respectful to everyone whom you encounter from the organization. Receptionists may play an informal role in the hiring process.

Questions ... A Two-Way Street

Questions You May Be Asked During an Interview

1. Tell us about yourself, your background, your education, and your career history.

2. What words best describe you? How would your colleagues describe you?

3. Describe a significant accomplishment of yours from the past year. What was the situation, what action did you take, and what were the results?

4. Describe a situation that demonstrates your ability to adapt to changes at work.

5. Describe a difficult work situation that you have had to deal with. How did you handle it?

6. What are your strengths? What do you consider to be your areas for development?

7. Describe the best manager or supervisor that you have ever worked for. What made her or him the best?

8. Where do you see yourself in five years? What are your long-term career goals?

9. Why do you want to work for this organization? Why do you want this position?

10. If we hired you, how would you make a difference in this organization?

Questions You May Ask at an Interview

1. What are the philosophy and goals of this organization, program, or department?

2. What is the mandate, or what are the key deliverables, for this position?

3. Why is the position vacant? Why did the last person in this position leave?

4. If this is a new position, what supports are in place?

5. What type of orientation would I receive if I were offered and took this position? What resources will I have access to during my orientation?

6. What are the ongoing opportunities for professional development at this organization?

7. Where can I go from here in the organization? What are the career succession opportunities available?

8. To whom would I report? What is his or her management style?

9. What other health care providers work on this team, service, or program? What is the skill mix? What are the team dynamics?

10. What do you think the major challenges of this position will be?

11. What hours would I be required to work in this position? Is there an opportunity to create flexible working hours at this organization?

Providing References

Employers usually ask for references once they have determined that you are a final contender for a position. Depending on the position, you will likely be asked to provide the names of three people you have worked for or with in the past five years. You do not need to use your current manager as a reference, especially if you have not advised your current employer that you are searching for alternative work. Instead, you can choose a previous employer who will provide you with an excellent reference. Be aware that should you be offered the position, it may be conditional on a positive reference from your current employer. The people you choose to vouch for you should be able to enhance the information you provided in your interview. Be sure to get permission from the individuals you list, and to let each one know that they may receive a call from your potential employer. When you do this, describe the position for which you have applied, describe the content of the interview, and review what areas you would like your referee to highlight when they are called. Give the individuals as much information as possible so they can speak knowledgeably and positively about your abilities.

Coaching and Mentoring—Key Elements

At some stage in your career you may use a coach or have a mentor. Alternatively, you may become a coach or a mentor yourself. Coaching and mentoring are independent but related communication strategies; they promote professional development and career satisfaction in the short term, and influence retention in the longer term. Although coaching and mentoring have many similarities, understanding their differences will help you to ensure that you choose the right strategy to help you, and for the right purpose.

Coaching is a collaborative relationship undertaken between a coach and a willing individual, the client. Coaching is time-limited and focused, and uses conversation to help clients achieve their goals. It is also goal- and solution-directed. Mentoring, however, is a longer-term relationship in which someone with more experience and wisdom supports and encourages another as that individual grows and develops both professionally and personally. The focus in mentoring is on an individual's overall development, and the relationship is usually open-ended in time. Given that both coaching and mentoring are about communication, it is clear that excellent coaches and excellent mentors share many of the same attributes. However, while both roles require superior interpersonal and communication skills, coaching is a focused activity that demands skill in generating meaningful conversations and letting the client "lead." On the other hand, the emphasis in mentoring is on the relationship between the mentor and protegé, and on the ongoing development of the protegé, a person who receives help, guidance, and support from someone with more experience or influence. Also, mentoring relies heavily on the wisdom, maturity, and experience of the mentor.

Although coaching and mentoring are aligned, they are independent strategies governed by differing concepts. What unites them is that both, if they are to be successful, are founded upon mutual trust and respect, and on excellent communication skills.

Selected Further Reading

Here's a tip: Check online or at your local library or bookstore for current career planning and development resources. The following are good reads from our bookshelves:

Beatty, R. (2003). *The interview kit.* New York: John Wiley & Sons.

Beatty, R. (2003). *The resume kit.* New York: John Wiley & Sons.

Bolles, R.N. (2008). *What color is your parachute? A practical manual for job-hunters and career-changers.* Berkeley, CA: Ten Speed Press.

Bridges, W. (2004). *Transitions: Making sense of life's changes.* Reading, MA: Addison-Wesley.

Bronson, P. (2002). *What should I do with my life?* New York: Random House.

Buckingham, M. (2007). *Go put your strengths to work.* New York: Simon & Schuster.

Coombs, A. (2001). *The living workplace.* Toronto: HarperCollins.

Craig, R. (2004). *Leaving the mother ship.* Toronto: Knowledge to Action Press.

Darling, D. (2003). *The networking survival guide: Get the success you want by tapping into the people you know.* New York: McGraw Hill.

Dikel, M. & Roehm, F. (2006). *Guide to Internet job searching.* New York: McGraw-Hill.

Donner, G., & Wheeler, M. (Eds.). (2004). *Taking control of your nursing career* (2nd ed.). Toronto: Elsevier.

Donner, G., & Wheeler, M. (2007). *A guide to coaching and mentoring in nursing.* Geneva: International Council of Nurses.

Donner, G., & Wheeler, M. (in press). *Coaching in nursing workbook.* Online. Geneva: International Council of Nurses.

Dychtwald, K. & Kadlec, D. (2005). *The power years: A user's guide to the rest of your life.* New Jersey: John Wiley & Sons.

Edwards, P., & Edwards, S. (2000). *The practical dreamer's handbook.* New York: Putnam.

Erickson Walker, J. (2000). *The age advantage: Making the most of your mid-life career transition.* New York: Berkley Books.

Handy, C. (2005). *Understanding organizations.* New York: Penguin Global.

Jones, L. (1998). *The path: Creating your mission statement for work and for life.* New York: Hyperion.

Kanchier, C. (2000). *Dare to change your job and your life.* Indianapolis: JIST Works.

Misner, I. (2000). *Masters of networking: Building relationships for your pocketbook and soul.* Marietta, Georgia: Bard Press.

Moses, B. (2000). *The good news about careers: How you'll be working in the next decade.* Toronto: Jossey-Bass.

Rath, T. (2007). *StrengthsFinder 2.0.* New York: Gallup Press.

Schein, E. (2006). *Career anchors: Self-assessment.* San Francisco: John Wiley & Sons.

Shaef, A. (1990). *The addictive organization.* New York: HarperCollins.

Sher, B. & Gottlieb, A. (2003). *Wishcraft: How to get what you really want.* New York: Dell.

Simonsen, P. (2000). *Career compass: Navigating your career strategically in the new century.* Paolo Alto, CA: Davies-Black.

Sinetar, M. (1995). *To build the life you want, create the work you love.* New York: St. Martin's Press.

Index

academic appointments, CV
    component, 86, 109
access to information, 7, 10
accomplishments
    articulating, 38, 43, 52
    CV component, 109–11
    and résumé, 85, 86, 105
accountability, 13, 78, 88
action plans
    feedback and, 55
    visioning and, 60
    (*See also* career plan—sustaining;
        strategic action plan)
action steps, 75
activities
    career vision, 62–65
    feedback, 53–54
    goal setting, 74–75
    marketing, 91
    scanning, 33–36
    self-assessment, 44–52
    self-limiting beliefs, 67
    strategic career plan, 77, 79
adaptability, 41, 61
advisory committees, 90
acute care patients, 10–11
aging
    healthy, 23
    population, 9
    professionals. *See* older
        professionals
anti-virus protection, 108
appreciation
    of inner resources, 55
notes, 53
assessing
    interests, 42
    knowledge/skills, 41
    values, 40–42
    (*See also* self-assessment)
assessment services, 103
assessment tools, 101–3

awards
    CV component, 86, 109
    résumé component, 107

backup plans, 74
backup files, 108
balance. See work–life balance
barriers, perceived vs. real, 66 (*See also*
    self-limiting beliefs)
"beginner," defined, 18 (*See also*
    early-career professionals)
behavioural questions, interviews, 89
beliefs
    changes in, 55
    self-limiting, 66
blogs, 87–88
blue-sky thinking, 62
boards/committees, CV component,
    110–11
business cards, 87

Campbell Interest and Skill Survey
    (CISS), 102
career centres, 76, 103
career coaching, 89, 98–99, 101, 103
    compared with mentoring, 117–18
career continuity, 105, 106 (*See also*
    résumés)
career continuum
    defined, 2
    early-career professionals, 17–19
    late-career professionals, 21–23
    mid-career professionals, 19–21
career continuum—stages
    commitment, 16
    consolidation, 16–17
    entry, 16
    learning, 15
    withdrawal, 17
career direction
    assessment tools, 102
    model, 20–21

career objective, résumé, 106
Career Occupational Preference System (COPS), 102
Career Orientation Placement and Evaluation Survey (COPE), 102
career plan
  documenting, 73
  and goal setting, 73–75
career plan—sustaining, 97–100
  assessment tools, 101–3
  coaching/mentoring, 117–18
  CV outline, 109–11
  interview tips, 113–16
  resources, 119–21
  résumé tips, 105–8
  (See also strategic career plan)
career planning
  benefits of, 3
  functions of, 3
career readiness checklist, 27–28, 94–95
career support team, 98 (See also feedback; networking/networks)
career transitions, 2–3, 5, 17
career vision
  activity, 62–65
  adjusting, 65, 68, 74
  creating, 61–62
  and goal setting, 73
  and strategic career plan, 71
  (See also visioning)
change
  acceptance of, 61
  acknowledging need for, 52
  benefiting from, 3
  and career planning, 3
  feedback and, 52
  networking and, 84
  organizational, 74
  and personal growth, 61
  visioning and, 59, 65
chronic illness
  key issue, 10–11
  and work, 23
chronological résumés, 105
coaches. See career coaching
cognitive intelligence tests, 102
collaborative health care. See interprofessional collaboration; teamwork

colleagues
  networking and, 83–84
  seeking feedback from, 52–53
  support from, 75
committees
CV component, 110–11
evaluation component, 53
and networking, 84
commitment
  to goals, 72
  to vision, 62
commitment stage, career continuum, 16
communication
  between cohorts, 12
  and marketing, 81–82
  skills, 11, 32–33, 39, 41, 117–18
community health, 10–11
community involvement, 21, 22
  résumé component, 107
  (See also volunteerism)
community organizations, 99, 103
community service, CV component, 11
competence, 21
complacency, 20
computers, 10
conferences, 84, 90
confidence, 55, 57, 83, 98
confidentiality, 10
congruency
  coaching relationship, 99
  current work, 42
  employer/employee values, 13, 41
consolidation, career continuum, 16–17, 19
constructive feedback, 52
consultancy, CV component, 110
consumer vs. health care costs, 10
contact information
  CV, 109
  résumé, 106
contingency plans, 74
continuous learning, 13, 16–17, 38, 41
contributions/legacy, 19, 21
control, sense of, 38, 74, 76, 78, 82
coordination skills, 41
cover letter, 86
creativity
  career vision, 63
  strategic career plan, 73
cultural diversity, 9

current position, CV component, 109
curriculum vitae (CV)
    components of, 109–11
    vs. résumés, 86–87
custodial care, 10

data, interest category, 42
daydreaming, 62 (*See also* visioning)
decision making
    and goal setting, 73
    and self-assessment, 38–39, 41
    and strategic career plan, 72
defeatism, 66
demographics
    and community health, 10
    and work shortages, 9
diagnostics, 10
disappointment, 52, 75
disease
    key issue, 10–11
    technology and, 10
diversity. *See* cultural diversity;
        multi-generational diversity
documentation
    career strategies, 71, 73
    personal/professional history, 55
    vision, 62, 63–64
Donner-Wheeler Career Planning and
        Development Model, 5, 23, 99
    assessing, 37
    career readiness checklist, 27–28
    marketing, 81–93
    planning, 71–79
    scanning, 31–36
    visioning, 59–69
dreams. *See* visioning

early-career professionals, 17–19, 60
education
    assessing, 41
    and career continuum, 15
    CV component, 109
    continuous, 13
    interprofessional, 12–13
    résumé component, 106–7
electronic résumés, 86, 108
emotional intelligence tests, 102
employee assistance programs, 103
employer–employee relationship, 13,
    18, 41, 116

entrepreneurship, 2, 22
entry, career continuum, 16
environment
    defined, 32
    knowing. *See* scanning
EQ–I (Emotion Quotient Inventory), 102
expertise/experience, 19, 20, 41
    growth/change in, 55
    marketing, 81–82
    and résumés, 107
    unrealistic view of, 52
extroverts, 39

failure, fear of, 66
Families and Work Institute, 11
family
    attention to, 12 (*See also* work–life
        balance)
    and change, 55
    feedback from, 52–53
    and networking, 83–84
    support of, 75 (*See also* support
        groups)
fear
    and career vision, 62
    of change, 61
    of failure, 66
    of leadership role, 66
    and pro-active approach, 66
    of success, 66
feedback
    activity, 53–54
    and assessment, 37, 101
    benefits of, 52
    component of, 53
    following job interview, 89
    reasons for, 52
    sources, 52–53
    and support groups, 98
finances, 18, 22, 23, 40
fit. *See* congruency
five-year projections, 18
flat organizations, 21
flexibility, 74
follow-up
    and career plan, 78
    and career vision, 69
    feedback, 53
formal feedback, 52
formal presentations, 90

forums, 90
friends, feedback from, 52–53
fulfillment, 42, 50, 55
functional résumés, 105–6
funded research, CV component, 110

generational diversity, 9, 11–12
globalization, 9
goal setting, 3
    and career vision, 73
    and risk assessment, 73
    and self-assessment, 53, 55
    and strategic career plan, 71–72
goal statement, 74–75
goals
    defined, 73, 74
    long-term, 74
    multiple, 74
    realistic, 74
    re-evaluating, 74
    short-term, 74
    vague, 75
grants, CV component, 86

happiness, 40, 41, 42, 76
hard skills, 41
health care — key issues
    chronic illness, 10–11
    human resources, 8–9
    interprofessional education/practice,
        12–13
    multi-generational diversity, 11–12
    professional responsibility, 13
    safety, 11
    technological advances, 9–10
health care costs, 10
health care organizations, and
    shortages, 9
health care policy, 4, 19
health care profession
    challenges to, 1–2, 7–8
    changes in options, 2–3
Health Force Ontario, 12
health promotion, 10
home care services, 9, 11
home–work balance. See work–life
    balance
honesty, 53
honours/awards, 107, 109

hospital-based health care, 10
human resources, key issue, 8–9
hybrid résumés, 106

ideal day, 62 (See also visioning)
ideal vision, 63–64
ideas
    interest category, 42
    and self-limiting beliefs, 66
identity, assessing. See self-assessment
image, 82–83
individuality, 61
imagination, 60, 63 (See also visioning)
informal feedback, 52
informal presentations, 90
information sharing, 83
information technology, 11
input. See feedback
Institute of Medicine (U.S.), 11
intellectual challenge, 40
intelligence, appreciating, 55
interests
    appreciating, 55
    assessing, 42, 102
    and blogging, 87–88
    categories, 42
    change in, 55
    networking and, 83
    self-assessment activity, 47–50
    visioning and, 59–60
Internet, 33, 76
    assessment services, 103
    assessment tools, 101
    electronic résumés, 86, 108
    publishing work on, 88
    and self-marketing, 87–88
interprofessional collaboration, 11,
    12–13
interviewer, feedback from, 89
introverts, 39
interviews, 88–89
    preparing for, 113–14
    providing references, 116
    questions, 89, 114–15
IQ tests, 102

job opportunities/identifying, 38
job satisfaction, 21, 41, 55, 68, 117
journals, 33, 76

Kaye, Beverly, 20
keywords, e-résumés, 108
knowledge
    activity, 46–47
    assessing, 41
    defined, 41
    and writing for publications, 88

late-career professionals, 21–23
lateral move, 20–21, 23
leadership role, 17, 21
    fear of, 66
    résumé component, 107
leadership skills, 84
learning
    career continuum, 15
    goals, 55
    (See also continuous learning)
lecturing, 90
leisure, 20, 21
letters to the editor, 88
life experience, 41, 42, 55 (See also
    expertise/experience)
limitations, assessing. See self-
    assessment
listening skills, 32–33

marketing
    activity, 91
    checklist, 28, 95
    defined, 81
    importance of, 82
    and self-assessment, 38, 40, 82
    visioning and, 62
marketing readiness activity, 91
marketing—strategies
    networking, 83–84
    projecting image, 82–83
    publication, 88
    Web sites/blogs, 87–88
marketing—in writing
    business cards, 87
    cover letter, 86
    CV vs. résumé, 86–87
    finding mentor, 84–85
medical error, 11
memberships/affiliations
    CVs, 111
    résumés, 107

mentoring
    compared with coaching, 117–18
    key elements of, 117–18
mentor(s), 16, 17, 18, 76, 82
    acting as, 90
    benefits to, 85
    defined, 84
    finding, 84–85
    functions of, 84–85
    and job interviews, 89
    and self-marketing, 90
microscopic surgery, 10
mid-career professionals, 19–21
morale, 8
morbidity/mortality, 11
multi-generational diversity, 9, 11–12
multiple goals, 74
Myers-Briggs Type Indicator (MBTI),
    102

networking/networks, 18, 36, 75, 76, 82
    and business cards, 87
    defined, 83
    and mentor-protegé relationship, 90
    and outside ventures, 90
    process, 83–84
    (See also marketing; self-marketing;
        support groups)
newsletters, writing for, 88
newspapers
    resource, 76
    and scanning, 34
    writing for, 88
notes of appreciation, 53

observer vs. doer, 61
older professionals, 11–19, 21–23
opportunities
    to make presentations, 90
    and networking, 83
    recognizing, 72, 75–76, 78
    and self-assessment, 101
organ transplantation, 10
organizational change, 74
organizational structure, 21
outplacement services, 103

paper presentations, 90
part-time work, 22

passion, 55, 68
peer-reviewed activities, CV
    component, 110
people, interest category, 42
performance appraisal, 53 (*See also*
    feedback)
performance management programs, 53
personal history, documenting, 55
personal notes, 53
personality
    appreciating, 55
    assessing, 102
    (*See also* self-assessment)
perspective of others. *See* feedback
pictures, vision story, 65
planning
    checklist, 28, 94
    importance of, 72
    (*See also* career plan; strategic career
        plan)
positive feedback, 52, 98
positive thinking, 66
poster presentations, 90
potentiality. *See* visioning
presentations, 89–90
    academic, CV component, 110
    résumé component, 107
prestige, 3, 40
preventive care, 10
previous positions, CV component, 110
pride, 43, 50
prioritization, 23, 63, 76
privacy, 10
pro-active approach, 61, 66, 78. (*See also*
    career plan; strategic career plan)
professional development, 3, 4, 8, 13,
    41, 99, 107, 117
professional history, documenting, 55
professional organizations, 19, 76, 84, 99
professional publications, 76, 88
professional responsibility, key issue, 13
professional visibility. *See* image;
    networking/networks;
    self-marketing—in person
projects, evaluation component, 53
protégé–mentor relationship, 84–85,
    90, 118
publications
    CV component, 110
    résumé component, 107

writing for, 87–88
purpose, sense of, 19, 20, 60

quality care, 9, 11, 12, 19
questions
    early-career professionals, 18
    evaluating interview, 89
    feedback meetings, 53
    interviews, 89, 114–16
    mid-career professionals, 19, 20
    retirement, 23
quitting, 20 (*See also* retention)

reactivity vs. action, 61
reading skills, 32–33
realignment (moving down), 20, 21, 23
realistic
    goals, 74, 75
    planning, 55
    self-assessment, 59–60
    timelines, 76
reality check. *See* self-assessment
recruitment
    and professional development, 13
    and technology, 10
    and work shortages, 9
references
    job interviews, 116
    résumé component, 108
referrals, 83, 90, 103
reflection, 38, 78, 98, 99 (*See also*
    self-assessment)
rehabilitation, 10
relocation services, 103
research, CV component, 110
resources
    career planning, 119–21
    setting timelines, 76
    sharing, 83
    strategic career plan, 75–76
restlessness, 19
résumés
    cover letter, 86
    electronic, 86, 108
    types, 105–7
    vs. CVs, 86–87
retention, 9, 11–12, 13, 19–20, 117
retirement, 2, 5, 9, 17, 21, 22–23
risk taking, 61
    and career plan, 78

and goal setting, 71, 73
and support groups, 98

safety
  and interprofessional teamwork, 12
  key issue, 11
  and mid-career retention, 19–20
satisfaction, 4, 5, 40, 55, 68
scanning, 82, 84
  activity, 33–36
  checklist, 27, 94
  defined, 31
  importance of, 8, 31–32
  process, 32–33
scholarships, CV component, 86
self-assessment, 3, 20
  activity, 44–52
  checklist, 28, 94
  defined, 37–38
  importance of, 38–39
  and marketing, 38, 82
  resources, 53
  and résumés, 85–86
  revisiting, 55
  tools, 101–3
  visioning and, 63
self-awareness, 83
self-esteem, 57
self-knowledge, 55
  assessment tools, 102
self-limiting beliefs
  activity, 67
  defined, 66
self-marketing
  activity, 91
  defined, 83
  and image, 82–83
self-marketing—in person
  acting as mentor, 90
  interviews, 88–89
  making presentations, 89–90
self-marketing—in writing, 87–88
self-perception, 38
self-regulation, 13
situational questions, interviews, 89
skills
  activity, 46–47
  appreciating, 55
  assessing, 41
  career planning, 3

categories, 41
communication, 82, 89
  feedback and, 52
  health care, 39–40
  leadership, 84
  listening, 32–33
  marketing, 81–82
  mid-career, 20
  outside profession, 38, 46, 55, 107
  and patient safety, 11
  technological, 9–10
  transferable, 41, 105
  verbal, 89
  visioning and, 59–60
  writing, 82
soft skills, 41
special appointments, CV component,
    111
specialization, 55
standardized (assessment) tests, 101
strategic career plan
  action steps, 75
  activity, 77, 79
  defined, 71–72
  developing, 73
  establishing timelines, 76
  follow-up, 78
  identifying resources, 75–76
  importance of, 72, 78
  modifying/re-evaluating, 78, 80
  questionnaire, 79
  success indicators, 76
  tracking progress of, 75
strengths, assessing. See self-assessment
stress, 9, 21
Strong Interest Inventory, 102
success
  adaptability and, 61
  defined, 3
  evaluating, 76
  factors in attaining, 55
  fear of, 66
  stages, 76
  multidirectional model, 20–21
succession planning, 9
support groups, 98 (See also
    networking/networks)

teaching, 90, 109
teamwork, 11, 12, 40

technical abilities. *See* hard skills
technology, 9–10, 12
tension, causes of, 12
testimonials, 87
thank-you calls/notes, 53
things, interest category, 42
Thomas Personal Profile Analysis (APA)
    Test, 102
timelines, career plan, 76
training programs, 15
trends, identifying. *See* health care—key
    issues; scanning
True Colors (tool), 102
trust, 53, 99

uniqueness, 40
Up Is Not the Only Way (Kaye), 20

values, 3, 8
    activity, 44–45
    appreciating, 55
    assessing, 40–41
    changes over time, 55
    congruency, employer–employee, 41
    defined, 40
    and early-career professionals, 18,
        19
    and multi-generational diversity,
        11–12
    networking and, 83
    and résumés, 86
    visioning and, 59–60
    work-related, 12
    (*See also* self-assessment)
vertical move, 20, 21
vision
    and action plan, 72
    activity, 62–65

defined, 59
original, 60
re-assessing, 60–61
and strategic career plan, 78
vision board, 65
vision story, 63–65
visioning
    checklist, 28, 94
    importance of, 60–62
    marketing and, 62
    self-assessment and, 63
    (*See also* career vision)
volunteerism, 21, 22, 46, 84, 107

wealth gap, 7
Web résumé, 108
Web sites
    assessment tools, 102
    self-made, 87–88
wisdom, 19, 117, 118
wish list, 62–63
withdrawal, career continuum, 17
Wonderlic Personnel Test (WPT), 102
words, vision story, 63–65
work–life balance, 12, 19, 20, 21
work shortages, 2, 8–9, 22
Working Style Analysis (WSA), 102
working styles, 18, 39, 102
workshops, 76, 84, 90
writing
    CVs vs. résumés, 86–87
    for publication, 88
    résumés , 85–86
    Web sites, 87–88

younger professionals, 11–12
YMCA, 103
YWCA, 103